Three Big Words

by
Stevie Ray

Punchline Publications

Copyright © 2015 by Stephen M. Rentfrow
All rights reserved.
Printed in the United States of America.

No part of this book may be used or reproduced in any manner whatsoever without the written permission of the publisher except that portions may be used in broadcast or printed commentary or review when attributed fully to the author and publication by name.
For information address:

Punchline Publications
10700 Cambridge Ct.
Burnsville, MN 55337

Cover design by:
Dragan Bilic
Vrsac, Serbia

Punchline Publications is a division of
Stevie Ray's Improv Company
www.stevierays.org

"Making it up as we go since 1989"

Acknowledgements:

Pamela Mayne, co-founder of Stevie Ray's Improv Company and a great friend. The Three Big Words wouldn't exist if not for her. One day I was talking to Pamela about a client who was requesting many more meetings than usual to prepare for an upcoming workshop. After hearing my confusion over the situation, Pamela said, "Steve, they obviously need more help than you first thought. Help them!" That single insight resulted in this book.

Gary Jader, a former member of the Board of Directors for Stevie Ray's Improv Company, mentor, and friend. His advice helped form many of the foundations of the Three Big Words philosophy.

Matthew Kraft, Managing Director of Stevie Ray's Improv Company and proofreader for this book. Those who know me know that I am a storyteller, and—like most storytellers—I tend to tell the same story over and over. Thanks for comments like, "You told this story earlier in the book!"

Finally, everyone who has participated in the Three Big Words program and continually strive to do their best for the people they serve.

This book is dedicated to:
My wife, Kanitta. Thank you for your companionship, laughter, debates, counsel, encouragement, love, and everything that comes when two imperfect people are perfect together.

Step-daughter, Ondine. Thank you for keeping me humble, for punching me in the stomach when I'm not expecting it, for reminding me that I am ancient, and for letting me be a part of your wonderful life.

Contents

Preface	2

PART ONE: THE CHALLENGE

Emma	8
Customer Service: A Weak Goal	16
The Three Deadly Sins	30
Stop Stressing Me Out	46

PART TWO: THE EXPERIENCE

Focus: Why Do You Exist?	66
Define: The Three Big Words	100
Implement: Simple Acts	116
Hire: Who Gets In the Club House?	136
Train: Whose Job Is This Anyway?	150
Coach: Lead by Example	170
Track: How Do We Know This Is Working?	186
Maintain: Don't Be the Flavor of the Month	202

Final Thoughts	222

Preface

In the movie, *Up in the Air*, the character of Ryan Bingham, played by George Clooney, travels for a living. A lot. Toward the end of the movie he reaches a personal milestone, ten million miles with the same airline. His accomplishment is announced mid-flight by the flight attendant to the applause of a plane-load of passengers. When Maynard Finch, the Chief Pilot, comes to Ryan's seat to personally congratulate him, Finch hands him a platinum membership card and says, "Seventh card we've made. Small club. We really appreciate your loyalty."

If there is one thing every organization craves, and probably lacks the most, it is loyalty; from customers as well as employees. Thirty years ago the term *Loyalty Program* was non-existent. Today, companies scramble to create new and inventive ways to keep customers from buying the least expensive item they can find in an online search. With the ever-increasing cost of replacing employees, keeping staff members from jumping ship for a tastier carrot is top-of-mind for companies as well.

I have been a corporate trainer for over twenty five years, for every industry you can imagine—legal, real estate, retail, transportation, insurance, health care, food production/sales, banking and finance, and government. I have had the pleasure of working with highly successful organizations filled with happy, functional employees. Sadly, I have also been introduced to companies that left me wondering how they survive in spite of their best efforts. Stories abound about business blunders that have destroyed companies; over-ambitious expansions, over-stretched financials, over-confidence in the market, or a complete lack of awareness of what the customer wants. These errors are common, and deadly, but this book starts with the assumption that you know how to analyze financial statements and that you have a good grasp on market needs. This book doesn't assume that everything is perfect in your organization; neither does it assume that you are headed for a crash. I write with the assumption that you are either in a good situation and want to make it better, or you have some problems and aren't quite sure how to fix them.

Do not look to this book for tricks to keep customers. Tricks don't create lasting results. And if you are looking for a tips-and-techniques book; again, this will be a disappointment. This book offers a frame-work that has proved successful for many of my clients, but in order for the frame-work to work, you will have to be diligent and disciplined. If you are looking to this book to make things easier, you are half right. The steps I will suggest are like most good ideas; ridiculously easy to understand. There will be added work on your part to implement them and even more work to maintain them over time. If I did promise a simple solution you would be foolish to believe me. What I do promise is that, if you follow the steps I put forth, you will have more engaged employees, which is the only way to create loyal customers.

As part of my career I write a nationally syndicated column for the Business Journal Newspapers. Having written for the publication since 1997, I hold the distinction of being the longest running columnist for the publication. My editor told me that my longevity has prompted his staff to refer to me as the "Cal Ripkin of columnists." I don't tell you that to try to impress you. The reason I tell you relates to the answer I gave to my editor's next question. He asked how I was able to continually write about the business world every month for years without running out of ideas. I said, "I pay attention. I pay attention to how I feel as a customer. I watch people interact at the companies I work with. And I listen carefully during conversations with employees. I also learn from others who are really good at what they do. I pay attention, and pass along what I learn." The ideas in this book didn't just pop into my head one day; they are the result of paying attention to the combined experiences of business leaders, staff members, and most important, customers. Now, let's get to work.

PART ONE: THE CHALLENGE

Emma

I was leading a *Mall Walk* for group of department directors for the Mall of America (MOA) in Bloomington, Minnesota. We had just begun the process of redefining the experience for MOA guests and staff; a huge undertaking for a company that employs hundreds of people in roles including maintenance, housekeeping, guest services, marketing, finance, security, cashier, movie theatre, and amusement park ride operator (The MOA boasts *Nickelodeon Universe*, with close to 30 indoor rides including rollercoasters, bumper cars, and a full-sized Ferris Wheel). It is also not an easy task for a venue that hosts over 43 million visitors each year, consistently ranking it as the number one tourist destination in America.

The directors knew that in order to inspire their staff members to embody the principles I was to teach them, the directors themselves would have to experience them first-hand. So about a dozen directors and I were walking the mall to see what positive impact we could have on guests. I was asking them to create a proactive rather than reactive atmosphere with guests. This meant not waiting for guests to approach staff with problems, but looking for people in distress and offering to help.

Even though the Mall of America can be an exciting place to visit, it can also be a stressful experience. The building has over

4.87 million square feet, 32 Boeing 747 airplanes could sit inside the building. The size and scope of a mall with over 520 stores can be daunting for the casual shopper, and I challenged the staff to look for signs of stress among the guests and alleviate it whenever possible. Since I was the one championing the idea, it was only fair that I be the first to demonstrate. So I had the directors gather in a corner while I approached two women standing by an amusement ride. I told the directors that the goal was not necessarily to make guests giddy with happiness, just alleviate stress and show them that people are there to take care of them if need be. I told the directors to watch the faces of the two women before I approached them and again as I walked away following our interaction.

I walked up to the women, one of whom was middle-aged and the other on the more senior side of life. "Hi ladies," I said. "My name is Steve, I work here at the mall and I noticed you looked a little stressed. I know all about this place, so if you need anything, I can help." They both smiled and the older woman said, "Oh no. We're just waiting for my granddaughter to finish her ride and we're trying to decide where to eat. Thanks anyway." I replied, "No problem. Like I said, I can answer any questions you have. So if you need ideas, just look for the guy in the red shirt." When I returned to the directors they said that the women looked at each other as I walked away and smiled. They couldn't hear what the women said, but they lip-read them saying, "That was nice!" "That's what we're after," I said to the directors. "We won't likely make people so happy that they skip down the aisles, but we can alleviate stress.

And that is the first of many important steps we will work on."

We continued the Mall Walk, with each director taking a turn approaching guests, solving problems, and easing stress. One couple looked confused, and when Ed from marketing asked if they needed help they asked, "Where is the L.L. Bean store?" Ed started to tell them the mall address (every store is located in either the north, south, east, or west section and has a number on the store front to act as a locator. So a store might have the address *N202*). Some newcomers find this system hard to navigate, and some old-timers still get turned around. Knowing that the L.L. Bean store was a good mile away, I interrupted Ed and said, "Ed, you know the mall better than anyone. Why don't you take our guests there yourself?" A light went off above Ed's head and off he went with the two guests in tow.

After each guest interaction, the directors regrouped to share their experiences. When Ed returned he said, "I can't believe it. I started by asking them if they had been to the mall before and by the time we got to L.L. Bean they had given me a dozen suggestions to improve the mall experience." Fired up, Ed trotted off to eagerly help another couple that looked lost. Then it was Ben's turn. Ben is the head of security. Before you chuckle and think of the movie *Mall Cop*, there are shopping mall security officers and then there are security officers for the Mall of America. Like it or not, places of public gathering can attract wackos. As such, the security team at the MOA is considered a top-notch training facility for law enforcement and security. The MOA typically loses half their security force each year as their officers are hired at law enforcement or federal agencies around the country.

At first glance, Ben is exactly what you would expect from a chief of security; his barrel-chested frame stands six-foot-five-inches and supports a head with close-cropped hair and a square jaw. If you saw him walking toward you with *Security* emblazoned on his shirt and his beefy arms swinging as he walked, you would think you were in big trouble. To talk to Ben, however, you would think he was a camp counselor; jovial and welcoming with a quick smile. During our Mall Walk Ben saw a woman standing by a roller coaster and off he went. A few minutes later he returned with a big smile and great story. He told the group, "I walked up to her and said 'Hi. My name is Ben. I am in charge of security here at the mall. I see you watching your kids on the ride and you seem like an observant person.'" Commenting on someone's powers of observation may not be a typical way to start a conversation, but it worked. He said, "I then said to her, 'Since you are an observant person, do you have any observations about the mall you could share with me?' Without missing a beat she said, 'Yes. I see you have benches for parents waiting for their kids to finish a ride, but the benches are near the entrance to the ride. Why don't you put them at the exit so we can be there when our kids get off? And another thing; we use our cell phones the whole time we are here so the battery gets drained. There aren't any outlets for us to charge our phones. You know how airports now have charging stations? You should have those at the mall, especially in the amusement park.'"

The directors were abuzz about all the great suggestions that came from one random interaction. They said that their online surveys rarely resulted in useful suggestions. They learned a valuable lesson that day; conversation will always provide better ideas than surveys. Conversation happens in the moment, when the experience is fresh. Online surveys are not reliable for two reasons; people take them because they are unhappy and want to complain, or because they just want the incentive or prize offered for taking the survey. One results in ranting, the other is a rush to finish a tedious task.

By this time the group was a full-contact mode. They were venturing out to guests and returning with great stories and suggestions. I stayed at the gathering site so I could monitor the process. We had chosen an area that was centrally located within the amusement park, so guests were coming and going all around us. That is when I spotted Emma. In that instant the thousands of people in the mall were reduced to one child. The slogan of the Mall of America is, *A place for fun in your life*, but it was obvious that this little girl was not having fun. Emma was sitting on a low stone wall with her mother and father on either side of her. She was dressed in a bright pink shirt and purple pants, (just like a little girl should). Mom and Dad were in faded jeans and sweatshirts. I watched as they tried to console their tearful daughter. Ask they spoke, her blonde curls bobbed up and down as she nodded her head. It was the nod a toddler gives when they understand, but don't like what they hear.

I wasn't sure how to approach the situation, but I had just finished telling the directors that they couldn't take the easy way out on the Mall Walk by only speaking to people who seemed happy; they had to take risks and start conversations that might be uncomfortable. So, I told the directors to wait while I approached mom, dad, and tearful child. "Hi," I said. "My name is Steve and I work here at the mall." They looked up, surprised that anyone noticed them among the thousands of people. Taking a page from Ben's *Just say what you see* rulebook I said, "I just couldn't help noticing that you folks don't look too happy. I was wondering if there is anything I can do." The parents exchanged a quick glance, then the mother looked at me and said, "When we asked our little girl what she wanted to do today, she said she wanted to come here and ride the rides, but we don't have any money. So she asked if we could come and just look at the rides." At this point, the father looked down and mom's voice started to quiver. "Now that we're here and she sees the rides, she wants to ride them even more, but we still don't have the money."

I was stunned. I expected to hear something about how the little girl didn't win a stuffed animal at the ring toss game. Here was a father who felt like a failure and a mother who felt worse. I looked down at the girl and said, "Hi, my name is Steve. What's yours?" "Emma," she replied. I asked, "Emma, how old are you?" She held up four fingers. I continued, "Emma, we think this place should be fun, don't you?" She sniffed and nodded. I said, "If I promise to hurry right back, will you wait here for me? I'll only be a minute." She nodded. I ran over to my group and said, "Rich, give me three of those all-day wristbands." Rich is the Director of Operations at the MOA. Rich looks a lot like Ben, you could as easily mistake him for a linebacker or Santa Claus, depending on the costume. Rich had thought ahead that day and had brought along a bag full of goodies—ride coupons, all-day wristbands, food coupons, and coupons for other stores in the mall—to use as gifts in case anyone was having a tough day on their visit. For the amusement park, you can either buy coupons with a certain number of points, allowing you to ride a few rides, or you could buy a wrist band for unlimited rides all day. There was no doubt as to which I wanted for Emma and her family.

Rich handed me three wristbands and I hurried back to Emma. Channeling my inner Willy Wonka I said, "Emma, do you remember Willy Wonka's Golden Tickets that would let kids eat as much chocolate as they want? These are better. These are magic wristbands. Do you know what they can do?" She wiped a tear and said, "No." I said, "They let you ride any ride you want as many times as you want—all day!" Her eyes lit up and her mouth froze open. I said, "I am giving all three of these magic wristbands only to you. Do you know anyone you would like to share them with?" She yelled, "Mommy and daddy!" I yelled back, "Sounds good to me, but you have to do something for me. You have to give me a high five and the biggest smile ever." The smile was already there. She smacked my hand so hard it stung, then started tugging at her mother's sleeve to get to the first ride. A four-year old knows that there is never enough time in the day for fun, so you have to get started right away. Parents need reminders every now and then about such priorities.

As they jumped to their feet, it was mom's turn to cry. As tears flowed down her smiling cheeks she could barely utter "Thank you *so much*." Dad didn't say a word, but as they walked away he turned to me and gave the only thanks one dad needs from another, a look in the eye, a nod of the head, and a thumbs up. The irony is I had told the directors at the beginning of the day that our expectations of the Mall Walk should be realistic. I had told them, "Don't expect our guests to be skipping down the halls with delight." Now I watched as Emma clutched the magic wristbands tightly in her hands, grabbed her mommy's hand, and skipped down the hall.

Customer Service:
A Weak Goal

Why would a person like me claim that customer service is a weak goal? As a columnist, I typically write about my experiences as a customer. Wherever I go; to the bank, grocery store, hotel, gas station, or restaurant, I keep a watchful eye. I not only notice what the employees are doing and how the customers respond, I keep a check on how I feel as a consumer. I compare how I felt before I went into the building to how I felt afterwards. If I feel better after my visit, the staff did something to move the needle from neutral to happy. If I feel worse, there is a problem.

The reason I think customer service is a weak goal is because the phrase itself has ceased to mean anything. Few companies clearly define what it means to them, and most believe that once they reach a base level of service they have done their job. And plain-old customer service would not have worked to solve the problem that faced Emma's mom and dad. In my workshops I often ask, "What is the one distinctive difference between your business and your competitor's?" The answer is usually "Our service," or "Our people." I ask, "Do you honestly expect me to believe that you are the only company that hires good people? Everyone else hires losers? And just how is your service better than everyone else's?" The answers are typically:

"We deliver on time and under budget."

"We keep our promises."

"We are a one-stop shop for everything you need."

"If you don't like it, we will do it over again."

"We are *the* experts in our field."

Companies who claim these qualities as their higher ground are fooling themselves about two things: one is that these virtues represent excellent customer service, and the other is that these qualities are unique to their organization. First, these qualities don't represent excellent customer service, they represent standard customer service. No one says, "Wow, I got it on time!" and then tells all their friends, "You have to buy from these guys, they deliver on time!" These virtues are also not unique. With few exceptions, everyone delivers on time, everyone keeps their promises, and everyone is an expert in their field. Any company that doesn't fulfill these basic requirements doesn't stay in business long enough to be your competition.

In order to avoid the trap of being like every other company, you have to start thinking differently about who walks through your door. First, people who buy your product or service are not customers, they are guests. Customers simply buy things. They pick up something off the shelf, take it to the counter, pay for it, and leave. This type of interaction never produces a loyal customer. People don't remain loyal to a process. A guest, however, is someone with whom you have engaged. When you throw a party and invite friends, you call them guests, not patrons. A guest responds to an invitation hoping for a good experience. So, in a very real sense, when you market your business you are inviting guests to a party. Everyone who walks through your door is responding to your invitation and hoping for a good experience.

In my youth I played harmonica part time with Blues and R&B bands in Minneapolis. At most of the clubs, I got to know the staff pretty well. One night I struck up a conversation with the head bouncer of a large nightclub and I asked him, "What is it like being a bouncer in a big place like this?" He responded, *"We are not bouncers. We are hosts. None of my staff is allowed to refer to themselves as bouncers. A bouncer's job is to bounce people out of the club. What guest would want to go to a place like that? This club is about having a good time. In a real sense, every night we host a big party. A good host makes sure everyone has a good time. We make sure they know where everything is. We provide great food and beverages as well as entertainment, like any good party should have. Of course, there comes a time when some guests have had a bit too much of the party and they have to be asked to leave, but we sincerely want them to come back. So we respectfully escort them out and ask them to please come back when they are feeling better. If we didn't treat everyone like we wanted them to come back, pretty soon we wouldn't have a party anymore. I love hosting a good party."* I don't think I have ever heard a more mature point of view about the role of security. Getting your staff to understand that everyone they encounter is a guest who is responding to an invitation, and that each employee is a host, is the first step toward getting everyone in your company moving in the same direction.

In another important shift in thinking; customer *service* must become guest *experience*. Service is bland, expected, and uninspired. Service is insufficient. Generations ago, America began as an agricultural economy. A person's worth was measured by what he or she farmed or ranched. With the Industrial Revolution of the late 1700s we became an industrial economy; and worth was based, not on what was grown, but what was manufactured. Later, we shifted to a service economy. The age that followed, and was in place until quite recently, was the information economy. Worth was based on the value of information. Your worth was determined by how much you knew, and how proprietary the information was.

America is now firmly rooted in the *experience economy*. It is no longer sufficient to provide satisfactory service; good service simply entails is showing up on time and delivering as promised. If you think that is enough to differentiate you from your competition, start planning your *Going out of Business* sale right now. People don't flock to Disney theme parks by the millions each year because the park opens on time, the rides are operated efficiently, and clerks smile and say, "Thank you." People spend their money at Disney parks because the experience is unmatched anywhere in the world.

People do buy products to satisfy a need, but the need often has nothing to do with the product. Your product is merely a means to satisfy a deeper, more important need. Marketing experts will tell you that people move more quickly away *from pain* than they do *toward pleasure*. That is why most commercials start by showing you undesirable images (overweight people, balding men, someone in total distress because they can't assemble a baby's crib). After the commercial makes us worried that we are living lives that are tragically unfulfilled, they offer the can't-live-without solution. The next image is of smiling, happy people.

Going to an amusement park is just as much about avoiding boredom than it is seeking excitement. When people do something exciting—river rafting or riding a hot air balloon—they say, "This is great. I haven't done anything exciting in a long time." What they really mean is, "I have been bored." When people move away from pain they are seeking a positive experience to replace a negative one (even if that negative is only perceived). What this means is that you cannot rely on the product or service itself to ensure the best experience.

When my company had its 20th anniversary in 2009, we were brainstorming ideas for celebrating the big event. One of the company members suggested that, since we are an improv company, we should perform the world's first skydiving improv performance. If you haven't seen improv, a popular example is the TV show *Whose Line is it Anyway?*. It is a form of entertainment where the audience calls out suggestions and the performers create instant comedy sketches, songs, etc. based on the suggestions. We contacted a local skydiving company and arranged for four of us to perform improvisation while floating underneath parachutes. When I spoke to the company, they agreed to waive the fees in lieu of us sending a video to television studios to market their skydiving business. We agreed that myself and three troupe members would dive together.

When we arrived, the guy in charge pulled a switch and said they could only take two of us up for the trade-for-marketing arrangement; everyone else would have to pay. The excitement of skydiving was replaced by the anger over the bait-and-switch. The skydiving location was a one-hour drive from town and none of us wanted to sit out the event, so out came the credit card. Then the manager said they could only take two of us *at a time*. When I arranged the event I explained that we would need four people at a time in order to perform the aerial improv. On the phone, he said that would be fine, but at the site it suddenly became "impossible." At first I thought there was nothing to be done, after all I am not an expert at skydiving. However, one of our other jumpers, Dave, noticed that a party of six had gone just before us. Dave marched up to the desk and told the manager that two at a time wasn't acceptable and they needed to keep their promise. The manager looked at Dave with a blank stare and said, "Oh. Okay."

When we finally jumped, the skydiving itself was a thrill, but the staff still tainted the experience. As we expressed our excitement, the instructors had a "We've been through this a thousand times before" attitude. Even when we told them our idea was to perform the world's first skydiving improv, only one seemed impressed with the notion. As is human nature, however, when his buddies displayed apathy toward our plan his attitude shifted to match theirs. Like a lot of people who are experts in their field, the crew was fine with us as long as we fell in line and did as we were instructed. When we suggested something a little out of the ordinary it became more work for them; and a problem. For most people, skydiving is a once-in-a-lifetime event. Now, whenever the four of us talk about the event, we can't reminisce about the fun part of the experience without comments including, "But weren't the instructors a pain?" and "Yeah, and what about them trying to squeeze money out of us at the last minute." If something as sensational as skydiving can be tainted by a poor experience, imagine how easily the same thing can happen in your company.

The inability to distinguish between the product and the experience has caused many companies to fail. So your first step should be to think about what kind of experience you provide. Think of emotions people feel when buying from you. What do you want them to feel when you first greet them, and how do you want them to feel as they walk out the door? Focusing on the guest experience can make you see your organization in a whole new light. Obviously there are some professions that can more easily relate to serving guests: restaurants, hotels, and spas. There are others that survive solely on the quality of the experience: theatre, concerts, and amusement parks. The problem is that an employee can often feel like the service provided is a sufficient experience. They forget that their attitude will affect the experience more than the service or product itself. I have seen amusement ride operators with attitudes that made me feel like I was unwelcome at the park. And there are industries where the staff forgets the customer is a guest. When was the last time you got an oil change and felt good about that experience? When was the last time you went grocery shopping and felt like a guest? I call this the *Who Needs Whom?* Syndrome. If a staff member feels like he or she is doing the customer a favor by providing a service, the experience will suffer.

I was called to conduct training for the faculty of the MBA program at a local university. Jack, the director of the MBA department, met me at his office on campus. Jack is one of those classic Ph.D. professor types—a head full of grey hair (what is still left of it), a dark suit that is probably one of three he chooses from each day, and an office cluttered with books that are beyond the comprehension of the average human. Jack was made the director of the MBA program because he is smart, but also because he is blunt. Frankly, when dealing with powerful personalities (one faculty member is a retired US senator), you have to have a sturdy spine.

During the meeting, Jack spelled out the problem right away. *"The world of higher education has changed. The old model involved a wise old sage sitting on a mountaintop. Students who wanted his wisdom had to climb up the mountain and sit at his feet. He would dispense his wisdom and down they would climb, to return the next day. Because we professors have always been seen as repositories of wisdom, we have been able to sit and wait for students to come to us. The internet has changed all that. Online courses now make knowledge available to everyone, so simply having the knowledge people want isn't enough anymore. We have to dispense it in a way that makes the experience of learning better than what people can get online.*

"The problem is many of our faculty haven't caught up with the times. They think that because they are brilliant, students should flock to them for knowledge. They are brilliant professors, but some are too smart. Some are great at research, but they can't communicate in the classroom. In fact, I think one or two are patently incapable of teaching. Learning is an experience, not a process. [Author's note: William Butler Yeats once said, "Education is not the filling of a pail, but the lighting of a fire."] We need you to help our professors learn how to teach. Because the majority of MBA students are working adults—many of them executives—their evaluations mean a lot to us. If we don't give these people a good experience, the resulting bad word of mouth could cause irreparable damage to our reputation."

After more discussion and planning, I conducted workshops to help the professors convert from lectures to interactive teaching. Since my workshops were optional to attend, I asked the participants at each session why they chose to take time out of their busy lives to participate. One woman pulled a sheet of paper out of her folio and said, "I am here because of this evaluation I received from a student last year." She read from the evaluation, "He wrote, 'If I only had one hour to live, I would want to take your class.'" The rest of the group was impressed, some even applauded. She stopped us short and said, "No. There is more. He followed that with, 'Because you can make an hour feel like a lifetime.'" She said, "I am here so I never get another evaluation like this again."

As we worked to convert lectures and PowerPoint into interactive learning, we discussed how misguided some teachers can be. Many teachers assume that the information is compelling enough to make buying it from the teacher an easy decision. This is the same mistake as assuming that a product is important enough to make its own sale. Making a purchase is neither an experience, nor is it memorable. And teaching certainly relies on the experience being memorable to make it valuable. A favorite exercise I use for teachers is to have them form groups of three; each member of the group a teacher of a different subject. One member states a learning objective from his or her course and the other two must brainstorm ideas to teach the concept in an interactive fashion rather than lecture.

During one workshop a professor was stuck and said, "I want to teach my students how to create a business plan. So I have them try to invent a new company and make a business plan for that company. The problem is that when it comes to inventing a new business, everyone gets stuck. I don't want them to create a business plan for an existing company; that would be too easy." I replied, "Just sitting around trying to invent a new company is next to impossible. You have to make it experiential. Have three students play the parts of husband, wife, and child. Have them start in one corner of the room and pretend they are a family getting ready for the day. As they move around the perimeter of the room, have them act out various daily activities; getting dressed, eating breakfast, going to work or school, and so on. As they act out the various parts of the day, the rest of the students should look for ways to improve that daily activity; making it easier, faster, or more effective. This will inspire new business ideas. The best ideas don't come from necessity, they come when someone thinks 'it be cool if.' The Wright Brothers didn't build an airplane because people *needed* to fly. They built it because it would be *cool* to fly."

I conducted the same exercise for a group of high school teachers. When an English teacher sat with a physical education teacher and a music teacher, she said her most challenging learning objective was getting students to learn vocabulary words. Rote memory is difficult enough, but most vocabulary words aren't used in everyday conversation. The music teacher suggested that the students create a song that included the vocabulary words. She said that rhyming helps with memory, and the repetition built into most songs also improves retention. The physical education teacher added that the students should have to create a dance to go along with the song. Playful, physical movement not only makes a task more fun, but linking movement to ideas connects body and mind, which also increases retention. The English teacher was surprised that she never thought of such simple ideas herself.

Note: After a number of workshops for the university MBA faculty, the professor with the horrible evaluation returned. She pulled a new sheet of paper out of her folio and proudly announced, "This is the evaluation I now keep next to the bad one. 'This is my least favorite subject, but was my most favorite class.'" We all cheered. Experience had won out.

The *Who Needs Whom* Syndrome isn't always present because of ego; history plays a big part in creating the attitude. Physicians have historically been in the position of waiting for needy patients to come to their door. And, as much as educators have knowledge we would like to know, physicians have knowledge that could save a life; this makes the question of "Who needs whom?" easy to answer. However, even doctors have had to shift their mentality. Wider choices in health care has given patients the freedom to be more selective when choosing a doctor. The internet has provided the public with access to medical information, and even if that information is not as extensive as the training a specialist receives, it does allow the patient more input in his or her care than ever before. Not surprisingly, I have been contacted by health care organizations more and more as of late to help their medical staff improve communication skills. Sometimes the most difficult obstacle is helping the physicians get past the notion that their expertise alone is enough to keep their patient load full.

I received a call to conduct a workshop that stretched the "Who needs whom?" question even further. Libraries are usually under the direction of county governments. Anoka County is part of the Minneapolis/St. Paul metropolitan area and the Anoka County Library Association called to have me speak at a conference of librarians. When I asked about the challenges they were facing, it was a mirror image of the university professors. The committee for the conference said that librarians have historically been the people who sat behind a desk waiting for anyone who needed help. Most librarians have advanced degrees in Library Science, which involves extensive training in research methods, but most people still only see librarians as the lady with her hair in a bun who says "Shhhh!" when anyone talks above two decibels.

The truth is, the internet can provide access to only about 4% of the total information available in the world (yes, even Google can only access 4% of all information). A standard library can provide access to almost 50% of the total information available (these figures were accurate up to the printing of this book). Also, a library is a source for so much more than books and magazines. My wife prefers books-on-tape over listening to the radio, and she always checks out free tapes from the library rather than buying them. The services available at a typical library also include reading and writing workshops, internet access, book readings by authors, game nights, homework assistance, resume assistance, interview training, and even parenting classes; all free to the public. Yet, even with the plethora of services available, library attendance continues to decline.

The committee told me that the Anoka County librarians were, for the first time ever, being asked to step out from behind their desks and attend Chamber of Commerce meetings, business groups, and Rotary chapters to let them know all the cool stuff available at the library (for free, no less). Many of the services could actually help businesses and organizations be more successful. This was a huge change for the librarians, who had to shift their thinking about the services they provided. They had to realize that the public's perception about the *experience* of going to the library, as well as the librarian's own view of his or her job, was shaped by history. History has taught us to believe that libraries are boring, stuffy places and librarians are boring, stuffy people. At first, the librarians were terrified of appearing in front of business groups and chamber meetings. After all, most people don't become librarians because they crave the limelight. However, in time they came to realize that the only people who could enlighten the public and create a new perception about a library experience were themselves. And if they didn't get out from behind the desk, funding for libraries would continue to drop, and pretty soon they wouldn't have a desk to sit behind.

Providing an experience, rather than just a service, requires refocusing your energy on the real outcomes you offer. Before we discuss how to find that new focus, there are some obstacles that you need to overcome.

The Three Deadly Sins

The late comedian, George Carlin, had a famous routine in which he condensed the Ten Commandments of the Bible into only two. It was Carlin's contention that having ten different commandments was never necessary; it was simply a "marketing decision," because ten is a "psychologically satisfying number." After all, so many things are based on tens: the decimal system, top ten lists, and so on. He felt he was able to eliminate and combine the various rules; creating two commandments that covered all the basic concepts of the original ten. You can see the routine on YouTube.

In the spirit of George Carlin, I have condensed the classic Seven Deadly Sins—Lust, Greed, Gluttony, Sloth, Wrath, Envy, and Pride—into only three. For some reason, the human brain has an affinity for groupings of three. If you ask someone to remember ten digits, 6128251832, it would be very difficult. If, however, you grouped the digits into three sections; 612-825-1832, they could recall the numbers more easily.

My three deadly sins are not based on any religious doctrine or moral code. I chose them based on the attitudes I have observed being most destructive in the workplace and in life. They are *Ego*, *Fear*, and *Complacency*.

Ego

A healthy ego prevents us from wallowing in guilt, being consumed in doubt, or frozen by fear. It gives us the strength to step outside our comfort zone and try new things. However, an inflated ego prevents us from admitting when we are wrong. It keeps us from accepting responsibility for mistakes. In his book, *The Five Dysfunctions of a Team*, Patrick Lencioni uses the phrase "Invulnerable Ego" when describing people who are unwilling to accept responsibility for their mistakes. They either deny that any mistake was made, or shift the blame to others ("My manager didn't make things clear" "My teammates are uncooperative" "I was too upset after watching *American Idol* to do any work"). Ironically, in their attempt to shield themselves from blame, these people end up being viewed even more blamefully by others.

In addition, an unchecked ego makes it impossible to accept any idea that isn't yours. It makes it hard to understand why other people don't realize how brilliant your ideas are. Are you one of those who offers an idea at a meeting and, if it isn't met with immediate approval, you repeat the suggestion over and over? Saying it slower and louder, thinking that the other people didn't hear you correctly? The little voice in your head says, "If I can just make them understand what I mean, they will see the light." At times like those it is good to remember, they heard you the first time; they just don't agree with you. It is like someone telling you a bad joke. At the end of the joke you smile, but don't laugh, so they repeat the punch again thinking you just didn't get it. People always understand the joke, it just wasn't funny.

When teaching creative problem-solving, I coach teams to find useful nuggets and hidden value in even the most far-fetched ideas, so everyone's ideas should be supported. However, if you think your every suggestion must be implemented, you have an ego problem. At a conference of physicians, I asked the group to name the greatest barrier to innovation in the workplace. One of the doctors said, "My co-workers keep coming up with stupid ideas!" Imagine working with that guy.

Do you constantly interrupt others while they are talking? You may have an attention deficit problem, or it could be that you value your own voice more than everyone else's. During conversations, how much time do you spend talking instead of listening? There is nothing wrong with being a great storyteller, but others have a story too. I was giving an evaluation of one of the teachers in my School of Improv some time ago, and I told him, "You need to be just as interested in other people's stories as you are your own." Every time someone related something that happened to them, he had to "top" their story by having a better story. He also had to top laughter. Every time someone told a joke, he had to get a bigger laugh with his own. His ego prevented him from seeing that, after a while, people stopped laughing.

Are you able to compliment others without condition or reservation? If you are a manager, can you compliment an employee without having to follow the compliment with something that you feel needs improvement? Those with healthy egos feel best when they make others feel good, without requiring reciprocation.

Do you thrive on authority? When challenged, are you able to see the worth of the other person's point of view or do you see the challenge as a personal or professional threat? To be sure, authority is essential in providing a stable environment. We feel more relaxed when someone is clearly in charge, but the leader must exude confidence without being overbearing. Certain professions are steeped in authority. Uniforms were invented to make people in authority easy to identify and to provide an air of intimidation in order to foster cooperation among the masses. However, two different people wearing the same uniform can convey "I'm here to help" or "I'm here to control." depending on the individual's ego. Police officers, physicians, soldiers, and airline pilots wear uniforms chosen for them; executives wear uniforms of their own choosing—Armani suits and Gucci shoes. Do you crave a uniform because it displays authority or because it shows that you respect yourself and those around you?

I have been pleasantly surprised at how some uniformed professionals are able to put their ego aside and be human. I have actually been joked with more by TSA security agents in an airport than I have by some service professionals. If you can get a laugh out of weary travelers who just had to remove their belts, shoes, jewelry, and coats so they can be subjected to a full body scan, you have a gift, my friend.

When you are in a confrontation, are you able to resolve it through compromise or do you resort to authority to "shut people up and get back to business"? I have spoken to dozens of dysfunctional executives over the years who claim that they get more work out of their staff because they "rule with an iron fist" and "keep unnecessary blah, blah, blah to a minimum." These ego-driven people think their team is productive because everything is done their way. They don't realize that the team could be even more productive if they allowed full participation.

A manager at a financial services company told me, "I don't understand it. Every time one of my staff members has an issue with someone else on the team, they come to me. I keep trying to get them to talk to each other, but they rely on me instead. They treat me like I'm their mother!" When I observed their next team meeting, I saw why. The manager used ego-driven authority to exert control over the team. Instead of treating the staff like adults she treated them like children; solving every problem, making herself the lead on each issue, and micromanaging each interaction. If she wanted children, she certainly got them. If you treat your employees like children, you lose the right to be surprised when they act accordingly. The only time the phrase, "Because I said so" should be used is when a two-year-old refuses to accept the notion that Frosted Wheat Treats with whipped cream is not a nutritious breakfast.

How do you develop a healthy ego without becoming the next Napoleon? Ask yourself one simple question, "Is what I am about to do or say going to make the other person feel good, or is it to make me feel good?" Negative feedback is fine, as long as it produces a positive direction for the future. If your actions seek to satisfy your ego, best re-think them. There is an old saying, *You can either be right, or you can be happy.* Serving your ego may make you feel like you are right, but it won't make you happy in the long run.

Fear

I sat at a conference table looking at six tired faces. These were the top executives of a major food manufacturing company. They called me in to help fix what they called *The Three Cs* of their company, Crappy Corporate Culture. Everyone was there except Mr. Wade, the C.E.O. Stanley, the Senior V.P. of Marketing, began with "We brought in a corporate consulting firm a few years ago to help improve employee retention and boost productivity. Output on the manufacturing line has been slipping for quite some time now. We've tried everything: bonus incentives, re-clarifying goals, even changing the managers. Nothing has worked." Bruce from R&D chimed in, "Yeah, and on top of that we haven't been able to get a new product line off the table for as long as I can remember. Every idea gets stalled and eventually killed." He continued, "If we don't get something new out there pretty soon our competition beat us to it, and then we're out of luck."

Helen, the HR Director, continued the story. "So, like Stanley said, we brought in this consulting firm. Their specialty is digging underneath the policies and procedures and finding out what is really going on with the employees…" Stanley interrupted (because that is what we men do; *ego*), "When they were done with their research, they called all the senior executives together, including Mr. Wade. They said that after extensive interviews and fly-on-the-wall observation they concluded that the entire company is permeated with a culture of fear. As soon as they said that, Mr. Wade jumped up, slammed his fist on the table and yelled, 'NO IT IS NOT!' Then he fired the consulting company. That was three years ago and things have gone from bad to worse. That's why we called you. Our C.E.O. rules by using fear as a weapon and it is destroying our company." It was now clear to me why Mr. Wade was not invited to this meeting. This was only one of two occasions in my career that I turned down a client. It was clear that they didn't need me, they needed a psychologist, and I hadn't watched enough episodes of *Dr. Phil* to fit the bill.

From the first day we are sent to school as children we are told to *face your fear*. Famous quotes such as, *Courage is not the absence of fear…* or *The only thing we have to fear is…* are supposed to make us strong in the face of adversity, but it seems the only people in our culture for whom it is acceptable to acknowledge fear are children. Fear is one of the most debilitating of human emotions, and yet we pretend it disappears as soon as we get dressed and go to work, it is quite the opposite; fear is more prevalent at work than in most other places. It is sad that most people love going home at night because it is the one place they feel safe.

Fear keeps us from making a simple phone call, asking for a fair price, voicing an opinion during a meeting, or having an uncomfortable conversation with a co-worker. Fear keeps us from being our true selves.

Psychologists identify three zones of human experience. The most widely known is the Comfort Zone. We all talk about "getting out of our Comfort Zone, but few really know what being in that zone really entails. The Comfort Zone is marked by a high degree of familiarity with our surroundings, and high productivity because we are engaged in a familiar activity. The downside of the Comfort Zone is that very little learning occurs at this level; if you stay there too long, you eventually burn out from boredom. The level just outside the Comfort Zone is the Risk Zone. In this zone there is lower productivity, a spike in stress levels, but also a spike in learning. After a short time in the Risk Zone you return to the Comfort Zone re-energized, armed with new tools and knowledge. We should spend most of our time in the Comfort Zone, and venture out occasionally for a breath of fresh air, mentally speaking.

People may think that fear is caused by entering the Risk Zone, but that isn't the case. We are apprehensive about the Risk Zone, but fear is caused by the final zone; the Panic Zone. The Panic Zone is marked by one quality, *an imminent possibility of a loss of something of value.* When we are at risk of losing something we value, we panic. In a state of panic, we do not make rational decisions, we take the first course of action that will return us to safety; we return to the Comfort Zone. We engage in work that makes us feel competent. This is not necessarily bad, except the memory of feeling panicked causes us to avoid ever leaving the Comfort Zone again. The resulting lack of learning creates burn-out.

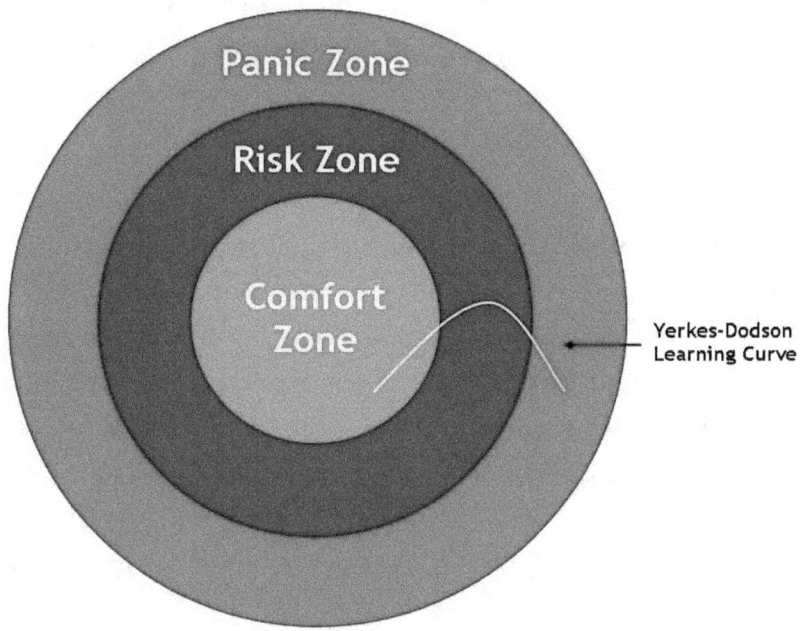

What do human beings value most besides food, water, and shelter? Self-esteem. Being highly social creatures, we are constantly aware of how we appear in public. If you threaten our self-esteem we will panic. So, by its nature, panic is most often caused by outside influences. No one threatens their own self-image. No one says to themselves, "I've been feeling too good about myself lately. Time to go out and take myself down a peg or two." We only enter the Panic Zone if someone else threatens our self-esteem. Good leaders know how to encourage employees to enter the Risk Zone by providing an environment where experimentation is encouraged; without the fear of criticism for the occasional failure.

Why are we so easily afraid? Why, if we know we are going to have a potentially difficult conversation with someone, do we mentally play out both halves of the conversation over and over in our heads? It is funny because the actual conversation never turns out to be as bad as our imaginary one. The reason for all this fear could be a painful upbringing, a previous dysfunctional workplace, or it could be simple biology. Recent neuroscientific research has discovered that we are wired with twice as many receptors for negative input as for positive. Essentially, our brains are still wired the same as when we were in the hunter-gatherer stage of evolution; with a strong need to protect ourselves from danger. Having receptors for negative input is a protective measure. The problem is, any negative input—harsh words, threatening body language, failure in front of others—sticks in the brain for a long time.

Having brains that are doubly aware of negative input can result in even neutral input being perceived as negative. If someone says, "Marie, you got a new haircut," Marie is likely to take that neutral statement and turn it negative; "Oh my God, she hates my haircut!" Input has to be extra positive in order to get through this negative wiring. Our brain has a remarkable capacity to lie to us. It will often tell us negative things about people and situations that just aren't true. People are, of course, wired in myriad ways, and some will see the positive side of almost anything. Neuroscientists have discovered that even our outlook on life is affected by genetics. About 90% of our social outlook is handed to us as a genetic gift from our parents. How happy, or sad, you view life is largely dependent on how your parents viewed life. The good news is, the brain is malleable; so you can adjust your happiness quotient up or down throughout your life with tools such as meditation, talk therapy, or medication.

Not all negative emotions, fear included, are bad. For instance, that inner-talk you have with yourself before a potentially uncomfortable meeting; the one where you play out both sides of the conversation? Psychologists call this process *defensive pessimism*. As negative as the term sounds, defensive pessimism can be beneficial. Not only does it allow you to consider all possible outcomes so you can be prepared, the process works to soften the blow if something negative does happen. The danger is if you allow defensive pessimism to override reason and listening. Allowed to go too far, and this kind of thinking can prevent positive relationships from forming or repairing damaged ones.

So what does this mean at work? It means that you can't just *know* that fear might be driving your decision making, you have to *discuss* it. You have to be willing to tell someone, "This conversation has me a bit on edge. Here is why..." or "I am frozen with fear about this decision, I need an outside perspective to clear my head." I have a friend who ran a youth camp. A favorite activity of the kids' was riding the zip line. The kids would climb a ladder to the top of a tall pole, grab onto a handle attached to a pulley, and ride down a long cable to the ground. The last child in line was Lisa, who was deathly afraid of heights. As she stood frozen at the top of the pole the other kids yelled, "Come on, it's easy." "You can do it!" "Don't worry, smaller kids than you have done it." She finally decided that she couldn't overcome her fear, and climbed back down the ladder.

My friend gathered the kids at the end of the day and brought up the zip line incident. He asked, "Who showed the most courage at the zip line?" All the kids answered, "The ones who rode it!" He said, "Really? You all did something you weren't afraid of in the first place. Did that really take courage? How much courage do you think it took Lisa to do what was right for her by climbing down that ladder, even though she knew she would be taunted for it later?"

If you choose your actions based on fear, you are crippling yourself. If you lead using fear you have discovered the easiest path to getting what you want, and an incredibly destructive force of nature. Williams Shakespeare said, "In time, we hate that which we often fear."

Complacency

Mammals generally live in one of two mental states: a state of comfort and a state of nervousness. All of our emotions stem from these two states. Being in a state of comfort leads to trust, joy, love, and acceptance. Being in a state of nervousness leads to disagreement, distrust, and distancing. These mental states are due to the fact that mammals are social creatures, having behavior dictated largely by the group. Humans are considered *ultra-social mammals* because we live in larger and more complex social groups than any other mammal. This means that humans have a third mental state, extreme comfort. Extreme comfort can be just as damaging as nervousness; because extreme comfort leads to complacency. Complacency leads to too long of a stay in the Comfort Zone, which leads to burn-out.

I was conducting a workshop at a conference. I stood in the atrium as the attendees filed in and I overheard one woman say to friend, "I hope this speaker is better than the last one." Her friend replied, "I don't care. I don't want to learn nothin' I don't already know." Sadly, I have often had clients tell me, "You might have a hard time with our employees. A lot of them are just putting in their time until they retire or something better comes along."

Complacency is behind the question "Why can't we just leave things the way they are?" It is behind the employee who rationalizes doing poor work by citing the poor work of others. It is behind the manager who hides in his or her office instead of getting out among the staff; using the rationale, "If there is a problem, they'll let me know." It is why people now rely on SpellCheck instead of learning how to spell.

Complacency is sloth, or as Thomas Aquinas said, "a sluggishness of the mind which neglects to begin good... it is evil in its effect, if it so oppresses man as to draw him away entirely from good deeds." Complacency is condemned in every major religion. In Christianity sloth is one of the Seven Deadly Sins. In Hinduism sloth is considered one of the five *Vighnas*, or obstacles in life. Hinduism claims, "Procrastination, forgetfulness, laziness, and sleep—these four form the coveted ship which bears men to their destined ruin." In Islam, Muslims will pray, "O Allah! I seek refuge in You from worry and sorrow. I seek refuge in You from incapacity and sloth." In Judaism, time itself is seen as a valuable gift. To honor the gift of time is to eschew laziness, whether physical or mental. Sikhism, Buddhism, and Jainism all consider complacency to be a waste of life.

Why do so many beliefs decry complacency? Perhaps they recognize how difficult it is for people to keep indolence at bay. As humans we are not entirely without willpower, but left to our own devices we will often say, "I'll get to that later" or "That's good enough." Laziness is the reason why I attend martial arts classes at a studio instead of practicing on my own. I know that having a class full of students will push me to work harder than if I was practicing in my living room. (Plus, my wife said if I broke one more lamp kick she would demonstrate her own karate techniques.)

More than the first two sins of ego and fear, we make excuses for complacency. Complacency leads to blaming our failures on the economy, the staff, management, ownership, or the government. If you blame the economy for every downturn, why are other companies within your industry growing and making profits?

I am a fan of the television show *Restaurant Impossible*. Each episode involves the host, Robert Irvine, attempting to save a failing restaurant. He is given a budget of $10,000 and two days to complete the challenge. His design team remakes the décor while he works on improving the food, the service, and the management. In every episode, he will invariable ask the restaurant owner if he or she tastes the food coming out of the kitchen. I am astonished at how often the answer is "No." In one case, the head cook had actually lost his sense of taste due to an accident, and the owner still relied upon him to judge the quality of the food.

Theatre owners are told to sit in every chair of their theatre and watch a production; not just for ten minutes, but an entire show. Have you walked through your building to view it from the perspective of a customer? Have you called your own company on the phone to experience first-hand a customer service rep? A well-known news anchor once told me that he personally reviews every news broadcast he delivers. This discipline improved his performance, which led to his rise to the #2 station in the country. Do you review tapes of your presentations, sales pitches, or client meetings? Do you have colleagues review your work? I have been told that one of the things that causes the most stress to a teacher is the thought of a principal or fellow educator sitting in and watching a class. Why do we all skip these vital steps toward self-improvement?

In an episode of the television show *The West Wing*, a White House staff member asks the Deputy Assistant to the President why it is so important that humans travel to Mars. The Deputy Assistant says, "Because it is next. Because we came out of the cave and we looked over the hill and we saw fire; and we crossed the ocean and we pioneered the west, and we took to the sky. The history of man is hung on a timeline of exploration and this is what's next." That sentiment expresses what American business must make its priority; what is next. Complacency leads to average service; to work that meets expectations, but does exceed them.

Complacency does more than hinder an organization or an individual. It keeps us from what is next. So, every now and then switch from FM music to public radio. Watch the History Channel more often than *American Idol*. Take the stairs instead of the elevator. Call a client or co-worker on the phone instead of using e-mail. Learn something you don't already know.

Stop Stressing Me Out

There is a reason why so many advertisements focus on stress. "We take the stress out of buying a car." "This is a no-stress method of weight loss." Stress is powerful enough that health care professionals believe it is the cause of most illnesses. Stress does more than affect our long-term health; it affects our decision making. As I mentioned earlier, people move more quickly away from pain than toward pleasure. The mere thought of a situation producing stress can cause people to avoid taking the action you want.

My wife, Kanitta, and I have a little game we play whenever it is time to try to return an item to a store. The game is *who should take it back?* Most people have an aversion to dealing with customer service because it feels like the rep's training involved everything that doesn't serve the customer. Service these days has diminished to the point where we assume we will get the run-around, no matter what. A case in point, we had purchased new wooden blinds for the office in our home. Kanitta had been after me for a while to replace the out-of-date blinds. Being male, I had to wait for sufficient time until I thought the idea was mine. In the meantime, she researched all the options and found a company that would deliver fast and guarantee their work. We read the instructions on their website on how to measure our windows and we watched their online video to make sure we were doing it right. The video was adamant about the customer providing the exact size blinds you wanted because they would follow the measurements on your order form exactly. I was fortunate enough to be raised by two parents who grew up during the Depression, so they were do-it-yourself types and they passed along that gene to their children. My father is also a highly skilled woodworker and tool guy, so I know how to work a measuring tape.

As you might guess, when the blinds arrived the measurements were off. All five blinds were too narrow, by as much as an inch. Since I was the one who did the measuring I lost the game of who was going to call the window blind company. After listening to some lovely hold music for a day and a half, a young woman answered. After I explained the problem she asked me to hold so she could call the manufacturing plant to see what went wrong. When she got back on the phone she said that, since we ordered inside-mount blinds (rather than mounted above the window frame), the factory adjusted the width accordingly. I told her that we followed the directions on their website and video exactly, that I knew how to measure a rectangle, and I wanted them to send five correct blinds.

After some tense conversation, she finally relented and said that they would send me new blinds, "as a courtesy." She then asked, "Did you want me to submit the new order as outside mounts so the blinds match your measurements?" Apparently, the stress of having to fight to get my order correct wasn't bad enough, now she wanted me to decipher their coded language.

I decided to use plain language. I replied, "I don't know what your internal language is for measurements, and I am not supposed to know. What I want are blinds that arrive with the exact measurements I sent you. Whatever code you need to use to make that happen is up to you." I can't wait for the customer service survey for this order.

In his book, *Stumbling on Happiness*, Harvard psychology professor Daniel Gilbert talks about the triggers that send the brain into either stress or contentment. In his research, Gilbert discovered that most people seek happiness the wrong way; they engage in fun and exciting activities hoping those will result in a happy life. He learned something surprising about becoming happy in life; the path to happiness is not in the pursuit of joy, but in the mitigation of stress. Joy is indeed necessary in order to live a full life, but joy is a fleeting emotion. The brain can only handle joy or excitement for short bursts, any longer and we would burn out. What the brain needs most of all is sustained feelings of contentment. Contentment, coupled with occasional bursts of joy and excitement, help us cope with the valleys in life; sadness and disappointment. The surest path to contentment, Gilbert says, is to get rid of stress. When you identify stressors in your life and remove them you do much to improve your quality of life, as well as the length of it. And a good thing to note when dealing with people, anger is not actually a primary emotion, it is a secondary one. Secondary emotions are caused by primary emotions. You may *be* angry, but it because you *feel* something else. The most common cause of anger is not disappointment.

Anger is most often caused by not feeling valued. Think about that the next time a customer displays anger.

Gilbert's findings should lead you to ask, "What are the biggest sources of stress for anyone dealing with my organization?" If managers spent their time seeking out and removing sources of stress for their customers; that endeavor alone would do more to increase business than the best advertising campaign. And the best way to discover stressors for your customers is to ask them. Too many businesses avoid this question, or they dance around it. Some surveys ask, "What could we have done to make your experience better?" This is not the best question to ask a customer. Most of us are not equipped to know what would have made the experience better, but we do know what made it worse. Henry Ford was noted for stating that he never asked his customers what they wanted because the customer rarely knows what they want. "If I had asked my customers want they wanted," Ford said, "they would have told me they wanted a faster horse." Effective surveys ask, "What was it about your experience that kept you from given us ten out of ten stars?" If you want honest feedback, you have to ask an honest question and not be afraid of the answer.

Ask a customer what caused them stress and they will be able to tell you in an instant. Stress is an emotion, so its causes are emotional. Let's say your website is poorly designed. The resulting stress is because finding something takes longer than the customer wants. The stress of returning an item is emotional, not because we might be stuck with something we don't want, but because we are going to have an uncomfortable conversation with an employee. That is why most people say, "Forget it. Let's just keep the darned thing." Stress is caused by feeling undervalued, overlooked, or ignored. The good news is, once you identify stress factors it is actually quite easy to remove them.

Look at drive-thru windows at fast food restaurants. It is no secret that getting a customer's order right isn't easy when you are trying to communicate through an intercom system that sounds like a radio from the 1930s. Getting your order right the first time is a big deal when you are using a drive-thru. If you wanted to leisurely take your time you would have gone inside. Some fast-food joints now have a video screen at the drive-thru menu board. As you place your order, the items you requested appear on the screen. When you are finished ordering, the clerk asks, "Is everything correct on the screen?" You get instant feedback and are assured everything is the way you want it. Stress goes bye-bye.

With the rise in botched surgeries in America, hospitals came up with a simple way to mitigate that stressor. Just before surgery, the nurse asks the patient to confirm the procedure being done. I have had a few knee surgeries in my life; in one case the nurse had me mark the appropriate knee with a magic marker. In another case, the entire team assembled in the operating room and the surgeon asked, "Steve, can you confirm for me which knee we are operating on today?" Being a jokester I said, "Knee? I'm here for a splenectomy!" (I walked with a limp for a while. Those surgeons have no sense of humor.) In both cases, the drive-thru and the surgery, stress was eliminated by including the customer as part of the solution.

Reducing the stress factors of working with, or buying from, your company is beneficial to both your customers and your staff. Whether it is a fast-food clerk who no longer has to deal with angry customers, or a medical team knowing they are performing the correct procedure, your employees being stress-free is important to your company's success. My mother took a job at a big retail store during the holidays when we kids were all still in high school. This particular retail store had a reputation for accepting anything, absolutely anything, for a return. You could return items they didn't even sell and still receive a refund. The board of directors knew that getting people into the building was the key to getting them to buy something. A liberal return policy was not only a de-stressor for the guest but a good strategy for increasing sales. One evening, when my family was around the dinner table talking about their days (remember when people used to do that?) my mother said, "A woman came into the store today to return a pillow. She complained that the pillow was no good. When I looked at it, she had purchased it a year ago and must have left it in a wet, dark basement because it was black with mold. It was so bad I had to use plastic bags just to touch it." We asked mom what she did and she said, "I gave her a refund." Being teenagers we were highly concerned with fairness in the world so we said, "That's not fair. She ruined the pillow. It's her fault, why should she get her money back?" Mom said, "Look, it's easier not to argue. And she bought a bunch of stuff before she left, so the company still made a profit from the deal."

I told that story years later to a colleague. By coincidence, he had worked for the same retail giant as a customer service rep when he was younger. He received phone calls whenever a guest was dissatisfied and the floor clerk needed someone higher up to fix the problem. I asked him if the job was stressful and he said, "No. All I do all day is send out gift certificates. When a customer calls I quickly enter their name in my computer. If they spend an average of $500 a year at our store I offer them a $50 gift certificate. If they spend an average of $1000, I offer them a $100 certificate, and so on. The store's mark-up on merchandise is enough that we make a profit no matter what I give away. And people almost always buy more than the amount of the gift certificate. Either way we keep the customer happy, and it makes my job easy."

A big stressor is uncertainty. This is why money-back guarantees work so well. My wife is a big fan of Trader Joe's grocery store. The reason Trader Joe's is so high on her list is they offer a 100% guarantee on every item you buy. You can return any item you buy, for any reason, even if you just don't like the taste. This is a fantastic way to get people to buy items they have never tried before. Removing the stress of uncertainty earns them her loyalty. As a result, Kanitta spends a great deal of her grocery dollar at Trader Joe's.

A professional speaker and trainer, Mark LeBlanc, helps small and mid-sized companies grow their business. In his workshops he discusses how good word of mouth is generated. When he asks his clients what they think generates the greatest amount of word of mouth they usually say "customer service" or "a positive experience." Mark informs them that the greatest amount of positive word of mouth comes from *the ease of the buying process*. When people encourage friends to use a particular store or company, they say, "You have to go there. They are so easy to work with." Customer service and a good experience are necessary, but the buying process itself must be stress-free. When I co-founded *Stevie Ray's Improv Company* in 1989, my father gave me a great piece of advice. He said, "Never make it difficult for people to give you money. You go to some places and they say, 'We don't accept that form or payment' or 'You have to speak to a different department.' If you make it difficult for people to give you money, they'll give their money to someone else." If you look the success of Amazon.com, it is not due to superior products, it is because they make the buying process easy. Also, in order for vendors to be listed on Amazon.com the vendor must be very responsive to customer complaints. Knowing that you have a big brother like Amazon behind you if you aren't satisfied is a big stress reliever.

When I conducted the Three Big Words program for the Mall of America and asked them to identify the greatest source of stress for their guests, the answer was simple; the MOA is really big! Just getting around a mall that size can cause stress. In order to mitigate that stress, we trained the staff to escort guests to their destination. During days of heavy traffic, the MOA stations parking lot attendants to point the way to open parking spaces. The simple act of showing people where to go—to a store or to a parking space—can relieve stress.

I conducted a Three Big Words program for The Historic Theatre Group in Minneapolis. The HTG operates four large theatre venues in downtown Minneapolis. These are the venues used when Broadway productions tour the country. As you might guess, the theatres are very big and very fancy. The stress? Crowds! With over 2,000 audience members each night trying to find their seats, use the restroom, or check their coats, the crush of people can be stressful. To mitigate this stressor, we trained the staff to recognize that the quality of the performance on stage meant nothing if the box office, ticket takers, ushers, coat check, and concession workers didn't display a calm demeanor so the audience would feel unrushed. When you pay a high ticket price to see *The Lion King*, you don't care how many other people are there, you want to be treated like you are special.

A final word about stressors within your company. It is common for staff to dismiss customer concerns because the staff is so familiar with the process. There can be an attitude among staff of "What's wrong with these people? This isn't that hard." Remember how the window blind company assumed that taking a simple window measurement would be easy; when in fact the lack of clarity in their directions made it stressful. Psychologists have identified *familiarity* as a major factor in reducing stress. Because your staff deals with the company process every day, it is easy to forget that it may be the first time the customer has ever dipped a toe in your waters. When identifying stressors within your organization, you need to ask the customer what causes them stress, and you have to take their concerns seriously. You cannot simply adopt an attitude of "We've got it covered."

Back to my knee surgeries, the most positive hospital experience I ever had was when, rather than simply assume I would trust them to take care of me, the hospital called a few days before the procedure to walk me through every step of the process and see if I had any questions or concerns. It may seem like a small de-stressor, but I have recommended that hospital to a lot of people since then.

Now that you have looked closely at what might cause your customers stress; it is time for the next step; adding a surprise. As I mentioned before, the human brain thrives most with feelings of contentment. (The world of advertising would hate people knowing this. It is hard to sell stuff to people who are content with their lives.) We do, however, need moments of excitement. Moments of excitement are even better if they are accompanied by surprise. Getting a bonus check is good, but it is even better if you didn't know the check was coming. In fact, knowing you are getting a bonus can sometimes be detrimental to happiness because you might have expected more money than you got. A surprise bonus, however, is wonderful. It has been discovered that a bonus that is a surprise can be much smaller than a bonus that was expected and still be perceived as a nicer gift.

I discovered this when planning to buy gifts for a couple of staff members. We employed two people, John and Kim, to alternate weekends managing our comedy cabaret. They had both been loyal employees and treated our guests very well, so we wanted to get them a thank-you gift. Since my business partner, Pamela, is the Artistic Director of the company and knew John and Kim well, I sought her advice about an appropriate gift. When I suggested restaurant gift cards Pamela said, "No, those are too common. John is into electronic gadgets and Kim is a girly-girl. Get John a gift certificate to an electronics store and get Kim a certificate for a spa." When I handed Kim and John their gifts, even though the dollar amounts weren't that high, they acted as if we had bought them new cars. The combination of the surprise, and the fact that we bought things that were unique to each of them, made the gifts more special. They remained loyal company members for years. Studies have shown that a restaurant manager paying for a random customer's appetizer has more impact that a gift of a free dessert on their next visit. Because the former is a surprise, it has more impact.

Surprise affects employees of all kinds, including those not in the cubicle next door. Surprise was determined to be a key factor in keeping employees motivated who were part of *distributed teams*. A distributed team is one that is not located in the same office or geographical area. With globalization and the growing trend of the remote- or home-office, keeping employees engaged who don't have the benefit of regular face-time is a challenge. The type of communication that works best for members of a distributed team must be both *random* and *frequent*. If employees come to expect communication on a regular basis, it loses impact. Of course, communication must be consistent, but if it occurs spontaneously it appears more genuine. Randomness and frequency of thoughtful gifts do the same to elevate a customer's mood as well.

Unexpected gifts or pick-me-ups must also have meaning. When I receive a free-appetizer coupon in the mail as a birthday gift from a restaurant it is nice, but not memorable. I certainly don't scoff at the gift, but I don't run to all my friends and shout, "Look what those great people at Bob's Bar-B-Que sent me!" Frankly, if what you offer as a "cool surprise" is being done by every other company in your market, you don't look cool anymore; you look unoriginal.

How my company uses randomness and Frequency.

We try to make surprises memorable at Stevie Ray's Improv Company. One method is a small, but very effective part of how we treat our guests after the shows at our venue; Stevie Ray's Comedy Cabaret. At most theatres, comedy clubs, or concerts, once the show is over the performers hover backstage while the audience leaves. When the performance ends and the curtain lowers, any connection between audience and performer is lost. Some theatres have their actors stand in a receiving line by the door shaking hands as guests leave, but this can sometimes look like the actors are begging for a compliment. Our decision to avoid the receiving line or waiting backstage stems from one of the core philosophies at Stevie Ray's Improv Company; gratitude. We are truly grateful that the audience chose us instead of attending a movie or other live performance. We acknowledge that the audience has many options, of which we are only one. Add the fact that Minneapolis/St. Paul has more theatre seats per capita than any other city except New York, and the audience really does have countless other options besides us.

To show gratitude to our audience, as soon as the show is done the troupe members leave the backstage area and immediately go into the cabaret to thank the audience, perhaps even sit and chat with them for a while. At Stevie Ray's Comedy Cabaret, the troupe members must get to the guest's tables before they leave. Audience photographs with troupe members are common. The after-show meet-and-greet has become one of the troupe's favorite parts of the show. And the audience is always surprised that a performer would take the time to greet them at their table and thank them for coming.

What is the side-effect of the after-show meet-and-greet? The average return rate for a comedy venue audience in the Twin Cities is around 20%. That means that only 20% of audience members will see any type of comedy show—stand-up, sketch comedy (like *Saturday Night Live*), or an improv troupe—more than once in an entire year. When we surveyed our audience we were hitting annual return rates of 45-50%. At first, we thought it was because of the quality of our shows, but the Twin Cities has some of the finest comedy venues around. Once you reach a certain level of funny, you pretty much top out. We couldn't figure out why we were enjoying such high repeat business, so we thought of something novel; we talked to our customers about it. We realized that, if we were already spending time chatting with them after shows, we might as well ask them why they came back so often. The answer was consistent, "At Stevie Ray's, you feel like family."

We were taken aback. We expected to hear something like "Because you guys are the funniest in town," not a reference to being a member of the family. When we started the practice of a post-show audience greeting, we didn't set out to make the audience feel like one of the gang, we just wanted to show our appreciation. After learning this, we began observing the audience before the show as well. We noticed that when a troupe member walked through the cabaret an audience member would call out, "Hey Brett! Over here." As Brett walked over to the table the guest would say to his table-mates, "I know this guy!" Then the guest would proudly introduce Brett to his friends. This kind of thing was happening before and after the show every night, right under our noses. One small gesture, that became a core philosophy in the way the troupe interacts with the audience, now drives repeat business. This kind of communication with the audience may be planned on our part, but appears to an audience member as spontaneous. And the length of time the performers chat with the audience provides a more consistent experience than the fleeting handshake at a receiving line.

Brett is actually one of our longest running troupe members. One night an entire bus-load of kids from a university theatre department came to see the show. As a surprise, Brett ran out to their bus just before it left the parking lot. He walked up and down the aisle shaking hands and giving high-fives. That little surprise was a bigger hit for the students than the show itself.

Another thing we do at Stevie Ray's Comedy Cabaret to provide a little surprise is how we handle special events. When you attend a play or live performance, if you mention that it is your guest's birthday or anniversary, the most you might get is a quick mention during the pre-show announcements. Performing an improv show gives us a lot more flexibility, and because we always look for ways to personalize our shows, we have invented a number of improv pieces that can actually have an audience member on stage performing with the troupe. So, just when the unsuspecting audience member thinks that a "Happy Birthday, Susie" from the host is all she is going to get, the host says, "Let's help Susie really remember her birthday. Let's bring her on stage to perform with us." The audience goes wild, Susie's face turns beet red, and her entire family pulls out their cell phones to videotape her debut performance. We structure the improv pieces so that Susie doesn't look foolish, rather she is the star of the show. Where do you think Susie will bring her husband on his birthday for revenge? Once again, spontaneity goes a long way.

The pre-show announcement at most theatres must include the stipulation, "No photography or video allowed during the show." This is true of theatres that are unionized; as union rules prohibit any reproduction of the event. Since we don't have that restriction, we make a point of saying, "Please take as many pictures or videos as you want during the show, just turn the flash off. The only request we have is that you post them on Facebook or Instagram, or e-mail them to friends. We call that 'marketing.'" We are constantly sent photos and video of audience members who have performed onstage, but we also see people posting photos with captions like "Just about to have a great time at a Stevie Ray's show." Sometimes the best surprise is when you tell a guest which rules they *don't* have to follow.

Kanitta and I received a nice surprise when we ordered some stuff for the house. We were converting some pantry shelves into sliding drawers. The online order form asked us to specify whether we wanted a standard wood finish or a more expensive option. Since the drawers weren't going to be out where people could see them, we chose the standard finish. When they arrived in December just before the holidays, a note was attached that read, "We gave you the upgraded finish at no extra charge. Merry Christmas!" You can bet that all of my friends heard about that company.

So you have some work to do before you even formally start the Three Big Words program. Bet you wish you had skipped

Part One. Now let's get to the steps of the Three Big Words program.

PART TWO: THE EXPERIENCE

Focus:
Why Do You Exist?

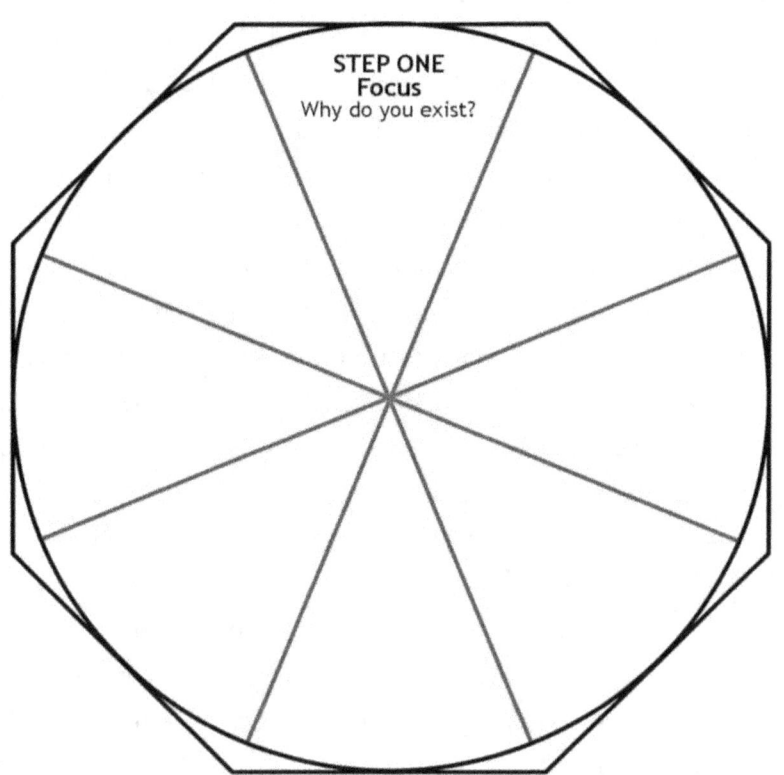

The first question I ask companies when I start working with them is, "Why do you exist?" This usually results in some raised eyebrows. Many leaders think that the reason their organization exists is obvious. A restaurant exists to sell food. A car wash exists to clean cars. When I conducted the employee training sessions for the Mall of America, I asked each department group the same question. I often turn this question into an exercise for companies I work with. I have staff members break into groups of four and each group has to agree on an answer to the question, "Why does this organization exist?" I include a caveat; the answer cannot be the mission statement of the company. Mission statements are a necessary part of a forward thinking company. A mission statement outlines how the company views itself and what it will focus on for the future. Unfortunately, most mission statements are too fancy for everyday use. Ask most employees and they can't even recite the mission statement. The real reason that a company exists must be simple, easily stated, and able to be quoted by everyone from the CEO to the intern. I always say that if you can't state the reason your company exists to a friend while having coffee, then the statement must be rewritten. Most mission statements are only remembered by those who wrote them.

When I asked the MOA employees why the mall existed, the answers included, "To be a place where people can buy whatever they need," "A place to shop and play," and the ever-present "To make money." In fact, one employee, an usher for the movie theatres, didn't even use words. When I asked why the mall existed he just raised one hand and rubbed his forefinger against his thumb in the *make money* gesture. The famous motivational speaker, Zig Ziglar, was quoted as saying, "Money isn't the most important thing in life, but it's reasonably close to oxygen on the 'gotta have it' scale." The CEO of Twitter, Dick Costolo, said, "We think of revenue like oxygen. It is necessary for life, it's vital to the health and success of the business, but it's not the purpose of life. You don't get up in the morning and say, 'I've got to get enough oxygen.'"

A restaurant may indeed exist to sell food, a mall may exist to sell goods, and a hair salon may exist to cut hair, but those answers do nothing to help me decide why I should patronize that *particular* restaurant, mall, or hair salon. Business owners who focus on trying to be better than their competition don't realize that the public doesn't live in the world of better or worse; they live in the world of "what do I need or want right now?" A fancy hair salon isn't necessarily better than a scaled-down salon, and a less expensive product isn't always a better deal.

More to the point, too much attention on why one company as better than another actually does more harm than good. When you say you are better than someone else, the customer rarely believes you. We would rather you simply told us what you offer and how you offer it, that way we can decide if it is right for us. Some days we want chicken, some days we want fish. Neither meal is better than the other. The one reason your organization exists should spell out whether you are chicken or fish. One hair salon's reason to exist might be *to make you look good, quickly and casually*. Another salon's reason might be *to make you feel like royalty*. Both will cut hair, but they will do it in their own unique way. The one reason you exist will focus your staff so they can deliver on your promise. It will also help you to treat your guests to a more consistent experience.

The risk of a company's service or product being seen as just a commodity is top-on-mind for many businesses. A commodity is something so common that companies are forced to compete solely on price. Gas stations are rarely a unique enough experience that people will go out of their way to visit their favorite pump. However, many companies still market their wares by focusing on the very elements that lead to commoditization; price, speed of service, etc. Rarely do they focus on the one element that eliminates the risk of being viewed as a commodity; the experience. Deciding the one reason your organization exists is the first step in de-commoditizing your company.

I was hired by a major pharmaceutical company to work with corner drug store owners around the country. The pharmaceutical company was sponsoring my workshops because they wanted to help small- and medium-sized drug store owners to better compete with the big three: Walgreen's,

CVS, and Rite-Aid. Most small chains can't afford extras like being open 24 hours a day, larger stores with more merchandise, and having drive-thru service. During the workshops I told the drug store owners about my own experience as a customer.

I had been going to the same corner drug store for years, even though there were chain drug stores that were more convenient. When I asked my audience why they thought I remained loyal to my corner drug store, they responded with, "good customer service." I would reply, "Yes, and no. The main reason I remained a loyal customer is because the pharmacist called me by name. He also knew a few things about me personally. My pharmacist always says, 'Hi Steve.' If it was summer, he would ask about my bees." The drug store owners looked puzzled and asked, "How did your pharmacist know you were a beekeeper?" "Simple," I would answer. "One day he asked what I was up to for the weekend and I told him I was on my way to check my hives. After he joked about having a good medication for hives, we talked about my beekeeping hobby. Then he made sure to remember this tidbit about his customer so we could have something to talk about other than whether I should take my medication before a meal or after."

My pharmacist did the smartest thing any business can do, get to know your customer's name and learn something about him or her that is unrelated to the purchase. I told my audiences that if they focused too narrowly on the commodity side of the business—price, hours of operation, etc.—they would ultimately lose. When I first started training in the martial arts, I would be frightened to fight a larger, stronger opponent. My teacher would say, "No matter how much bigger or stronger your opponent, you always have an advantage. If your opponent is larger, then you are quicker. If he is more powerful, then you are more nimble. If he is experienced, he may be set in his ways and you can be more willing to experiment. Whatever you see as an opponent's advantage, turn to your own advantage." If you can't compete with competitors on size, selection, or convenience, you can compete on experience. I told the audience that my pharmacist did such a good job creating a connection with me and fostering loyalty that if I was ever forced to visit a different drug store, I felt like I was cheating on my pharmacist. That is the power of knowing the one reason you exist and providing an experience. The title of my workshops for the drug store owners was, *Customer Service: It's Not in the Bottle.* Any pharmacist can count pills into a bottle. Real connection demands stepping out from behind the counter. Think about your company. Is the experience you provide directly connected to the service or product you sell? Quite often, the customer's experience comes from something outside of the service you provide.

I have the same relationship with my corner gas station as I do with my pharmacist. I don't buy my gas there because it is a one-owner shop fighting to survive against the big oil companies. In fact, it is a chain owned by one of the big oil companies. I plan my gas purchases around that one station because Ray works there. This station also has a nice little perk:

you get a punch card and it is punched every time you fill up. When the card is full you get a free car wash. A free car wash isn't the greatest gift in the world, but it is enough to make me plan my refueling stops accordingly. Having to go into the store instead of stand at the pump is another chance for the employees to connect with the customers. I had my car wash card punched so often by the same guy, one day I introduced myself. I discovered that Ray is an outgoing, funny guy (not what you would expect from the counter worker at a gas station). From that day on, whenever I stop in for a card punch, Ray asks about my day or what I have planned for the upcoming weekend. How many people can say they look forward to stopping at the gas station? With Ray behind the counter, I can.

Offering a singular experience is the only way to separate yourself from others who offer the same product or service in your market. And when you focus on distinguishing yourself instead of beating the competition, a wonderful thing happens—competitors become colleagues. I don't consider any of the other companies in my market as competitors. We provide similar services, but we are all unique in our own way. As such, I have referred many customers to my colleagues over the years. Case in point, the entertainment side of my business is Stevie Ray's Comedy Cabaret. As I mentioned earlier in the book, The Stevie Ray's Comedy Troupe performs improvisational comedy similar to the TV show *Whose Line Is It Anyway?* When a customer calls asking for show information, if it is obvious that they would rather see a different style of comedy than improv (stand-up comedy or a comedic play), I know exactly where to direct them. In fact, I have the phone numbers and show information for every other comedy venue in the Minneapolis/St. Paul area. I ask the caller if they are looking for a fancy night out or something casual, if they want a more on-the-edge comedy show or something on the cleaner side. I do more than just list information. By talking to the caller, I can direct them to the exact show that will provide the experience they are looking for.

Customers have told me that my providing information about other comedy venues made them feel more confident to use my company in the future. Some of my friends have said, "I can't believe you send customers to your competition." By viewing my competitors as colleagues, I follow the philosophy of the ancient Chinese philosopher general, Sun Tzu, who wrote in *The Art of War* that the first and best option is to turn an enemy into an ally. The one reason your organization exists should not involve beating the competition. It should focus on doing what you do best.

Trying to beat the competition is not only unattractive to customers, it does little to engage employees. Beating the competition is also only important to a few of your employees. In companies I have worked with, typically the only employees that are motivated by defeating the competition are sales people and attorneys; and lawyers usually confine their competition to the courtroom. And not all salespeople are externally motivated; some are highly competitive, but only in beating their own records. The rest of the staff is interested in doing the kind of work they do best, in an environment that suits them, with people they like, and for a purpose that is worthy of their time.

When I was a teenager my first job outside of delivering newspapers and being a Boy Scout camp counselor was as a busboy at a Perkin's restaurant in my home town of Rochester, Minnesota. Carl, the manager, was terrible at motivating people. He didn't think about the reason his restaurant existed, he only thought about two things: faster turn-over of tables to increase sales, and beating the other Perkin's in town in daily sales. The Perkin's where I worked was on the south side of Rochester. The only other Perkin's at the time was on the far north side of town. Carl referred to his rival as *Perkin's North*, and it was vital to him that we beat Perkin's North, especially on the most important day of the week, Sunday.

When I was a kid (before fire was discovered, according to my step-daughter), everybody went out for pancakes after church, so we were jammed with customers every Sunday. Sunday was the day Carl was the most animated. All day he would pass by the busboys, servers, cooks, and dishwashers with his mantra, "C'mon everybody. We've got to beat Perkin's North. Beat Perkin's North!" Given that most of us had no reason to travel to the north side of town, we had never even seen the other Perkin's, let alone cared about their Sunday sales figures. I remember the first time I drove passed the Perkin's North restaurant. I'm sure Carl would have been disappointed in my lack of animosity toward them. I remember thinking, "That place seems just like my restaurant." Suffice it to say, none of the staff really cared about beating Perkin's North. We just wished Carl would shut up and help clear a table now and then.

Another example of competition gone awry was at the Mall of America. The mall has quarterly, all-employee meetings where the leaders give front-line staff updates and company news. These meetings are a highlight for the employees; a festive event with treats and fun presentations, plus valuable information that helps the staff keep in touch with initiatives at the mall. I attended a few of these meetings to present the Three Big Words program to the employees. Before I spoke to the staff, some of the directors addressed the group. One of the directors was not particularly well liked. She tried to motivate the employees through fear and competition. She started off by quoting how badly sales had dropped due to consumers' love of online shopping. She warned the group that if something didn't change, online shopping could ruin them. Not a message that fit with the festive atmosphere the rest of the directors were trying to create.

Next, she tried to position companies like Amazon.com as the enemy; an entity to be despised as the mall employees went about their daily work. As I listened to this angry, frightened person speak, I tried to imagine a mall housekeeper, security officer, or ride operator going about their day thinking, "I have to up my game if we're going to beat Amazon.com." I couldn't see it happening. Competition should never be the one reason any organization exists.

Part of knowing the one reason you exist is knowing who you want to work with, and for. Companies that try to be all things to all people ultimately fail because they end up not being anything to anyone. I was hired by Cal, the CEO of a PR firm, to help him craft a short speech for a conference. His company had paid a lot of money to be a sponsor of the conference. As is often the case, a benefit of being a sponsor is the opportunity to give a five minute pitch about your company to the attendees at the big opening keynote. After his pitch, Cal and his staff would stand at their table in the vendor area of the conference hall. If you have ever been to a sponsored convention, you know the feeling of walking by sponsors' display tables. They look at you like a hungry hyena watching a tasty gazelle walk by.

Cal was justifiably nervous. He had to gain some new clients to justify the considerable cost of sponsoring the conference. I asked him a few questions. First, I asked if he had ever sat in a conference listening to a sponsor's pitch. He had. I asked him if, after listening to the pitch, he was excited to go to the sponsor's table to learn more. He was not. In fact, he admitted to circling around the room so he could avoid the sponsor's table. I said, "So our first goal is to make sure you don't come across to the audience like those other sponsors who you sought to avoid." Next I asked him, of all the attendees at the conference, who he thought would be the best fit as clients for his company. "We could serve any of them," he said.

I said, "If you claim to be a great fit for anyone and everyone, no one will trust you. Being the perfect choice for everyone is not a reasonable claim. We will avoid your table in the vendor's room." I told him that the more he focused on the one reason his PR firm existed, the more clearly, and narrowly, he could define his market. We ended up creating a fun, funny, and honest pitch; and probably a pitch no one in the audience had ever heard from a sponsor. He stood before the hundreds of people in the ballroom and said, "Hi. My name is Cal and I am with Cal's PR Firm. Let me put your mind at rest and tell you that I am not going to ask for your business. The truth is, and we all know this, that what my PR firm offers is only a good fit for about 10% of you. So I am going to quickly define the type of companies who are not a good fit. As soon as you hear your company described, feel free to ignore the rest of my pitch. Pull out your cell phones and answer e-mails, texts, play a video game, or just stare at me politely. And rest assured, if you are one of the companies who aren't a good fit, you don't have to be afraid to walk by my table. I will not pounce on you looking for business. Come by and take a free chocolate treat from the bowl and we can chat about the weather. Because, honestly, if you're not a good fit for my company I don't want to waste your time or mine."

He went on to describe in detail the exact kind of companies his firm worked with best. I warned him not to try to trick the audience. I have heard people say, "We only want to work with you if you are committed to excellence and success." Approaches like that don't fool anyone. The audience ends up trusting you less than if you hadn't said anything. The qualities that Cal described in his pitch were real; his firm focused on less traditional marketing methods, preferred working directly with decision makers rather than with large committees, and they were experienced in the food industry.

Most business consultants will agree that the more narrowly you define your market, the more people from outside that market will want to work with you. This can seem counterintuitive. It seems logical to assume that the more narrow your niche, the more you risk cutting out possible clients. However, people who are attracted to what you offer will find a way to fit your niche. The result of Cal's pitch, *everybody* at the conference came up to his table. He demonstrated a great sense of humor as well as honesty in his pitch. Who wouldn't want to hang out with a guy like that?

The one reason you exist must not just identify what you do, it must illuminate what is truly unique about how you do it. Many marketing experts refer to this as your brand emotion. Every product or service is bought because it inspires one of five emotions in the buyer; trust, competence, sophistication, ruggedness, or excitement. Your product or service can only be connected to one of these five emotions. If your product tries to be both rugged and competent, you cancel them both out. Every product, from jeans to cars, will fall into one of these emotional categories. A Jeep is rugged, a Lexus is sophisticated, a Buick is trustworthy, a Toyota is competent, and a Maserati is exciting. Knowing your brand emotion is helpful in determining the one reason you exist.

It can be difficult to choose just one emotion. Just like Cal wanted his PR firm to be all things to tall people, we don't like to narrowly define our emotional brand. However, clarity is crucial. Some years ago a marketing expert analyzed my company's website and hit us with the news that we were trying to be too many emotions at once. He said our corporate workshops were positioned as competent, our classes were trustworthy, and our comedy shows were exciting. He said that, unless we wanted to form multiple companies and market them separately, we would have to choose. With his guidance we realized that, although each division of Stevie Ray's Improv Company offered a different service, everything we did centered on excitement. Once we clarified this, we changed the language of our marketing and experienced better sales.

Try this. Ask a bunch of people at your company which of the five emotions best fits your organization. I'll bet you get a mix of answers. It is important that everyone be on the same page, and use the same language. I was asked to work with a large medical device company on this same issue. All 1400 employees were gathered in a conference center. The leaders wanted clarity so everyone would be moving in the same direction. I had the employees form groups of four and answer the question, "What is the one reason you exist?" After a few minutes I asked for some answers. One group said, "To save lives." Another said, "Zero defects in the medical devices we manufacture." Another said, "To become known as the best medical device company in the world." And yet another said, "To provide shareholder value" (guess who was in that group). I said, "These are all worthy goals, but something is wrong. What is the problem?" A number of staff members got it immediately, "The answers are all different."

Saving lives is a wonderful goal. It is a great reason to exist, but it is not the same as being known as the best in the industry. In fact, one goal can run counter to another. Providing shareholder value can sometimes run counter to zero defects. A singular focus on profit means decisions must be made that conflict with other goals. When that happens you run into trouble when it comes to making decisions. Debates can be more easily resolved by deferring to the one reason you exist. If there is conflict over which idea to implement, ask yourself which idea most clearly aligns with the one big reason.

Talking with staff members is a lot easier if you focus less on daily tasks and more on the one big reason. I learned this from an old friend and mentor. I paid for college by working several part-time jobs, including being an assistant in the emergency department at a hospital. I attended Minnesota State University-Moorhead, right across the river from Fargo, North Dakota (and yes, the people are just like those in the movie *Fargo*). I would try to schedule my shifts so I would work a Midnight-8:00 a.m. shift, go to school that day, then have off the next night to catch up on sleep, then repeat the cycle. I can tell you, performing CPR and treating car crash victims can give a kid a whole new perspective than the usual college experience. My friends were none too eager to engage me in conversation the morning after a shift at the ER.

I didn't buy a car until my last year of college so I walked to the hospital from campus. I once tracked the distance; exactly three miles each way. One night I was walking to work at 11:30 at night during a harsh Minnesota blizzard and thought, "I am actually walking three miles in a blizzard to get to work. Now I have to have grandkids when I am older so I can brag to them about this." Working the night shift had qualities that were quite different from day or evening shifts. Accidents that occur between Midnight and 8:00 a.m. are not the usual kid-with-a-sore-throat kind. Also, the night shift was staffed with only two nurses, an attending ER physician, a clerk who handled paperwork, and me. This meant that, if we had a busy night, necessity dictated that I was thrust into more direct patient care than a typical ER Assistant.

Having a more hands-on experience with patients didn't bother me. It kept things exciting. One thing that did catch me off-guard, however, was how often patients would scream and yell at me while I was trying to help them. Here I was, part of the solution, and they were treating me like I caused the problem. Being of college age, I was still young enough to think that being treated fairly was the most important thing in the world. Not being treated fairly can cause people stress and I was feeling my fair share. One night I shared my feelings with one of the ER physicians.

Being a Level II Trauma Center, we were fortunate to have board certified ER Physicians on staff around the clock. This may not sound impressive, but it wasn't too long ago that emergency medicine wasn't even a specialty. Emergency departments were staffed by a rotation of physicians from around the hospital; pediatrics, orthopedics, general surgery, what have you. The goal was to stabilize the patient as best the doctor could until the patient could be transferred to the appropriate department in the hospital. The first emergency medicine department in a US health care facility was at the University of Southern California, after the University of Cincinnati offered the first emergency medicine residency in 1970. It wasn't until 1979 that the American Medical Association and the American Osteopathic Association both voted to accept emergency medicine as a specialty. One of our physicians, Dr. Dave Ellison, was among the early physicians in the country to become board certified in emergency medicine.

Dave often worked the same shifts as me, so one night I approached him about my confusion concerning the patients. I told him I couldn't understand why the patients were so angry at me when I wasn't the cause of their problems. After I explained my angst, Dave thought for a moment and asked, "What is your job here in the ER?" I blinked at the simplicity of the question. "To heal people," I said. "To help stitch 'em up and get 'em back home." After he thought for a while he said, "Anyone can suture a wound. It's really not that difficult. And I could teach most people how to set a bone and apply a cast. The most important task lies outside of medicine. Our real job is to *help the patient recover from a traumatic situation*. An important part of healing is venting; letting the stress out. Accidents, injuries, and illnesses are stressful enough, add the additional fear and stress of being in a hospital ER and it can be unbearable.

"There are only a few really good ways to get rid of stress. You can go for a run, meditate, laugh, cry, or yell. A patient doesn't have many options to choose from, the easiest is yelling. They aren't really yelling at you, they are just yelling and you happen to be there. Your real job goes much deeper than assisting in procedures. Your job is to be a professional health care provider in a traumatic situation. The easiest part of the job is usually the task at hand. The most important part of the job is what you are really trying to accomplish." That conversation took place around 1980 and I still remember it to this day. It changed how I conducted myself in the ER, but it also transformed how I look at every job I undertake.

My managers at the hospital didn't know it, but that one conversation with Dave resulted in me being a better employee. I was pretty good up to that point, but I was simply meeting expectations, not exceeding them. After my talk with Dave, however, I didn't simply bring a patient to an examination room, take his vital signs, and go get the doctor. Because I learned that my real job, the one reason the ER existed, was to help people heal from a traumatic situation, I listened when they talked about their pain. I took a few extra minutes to make sure I was providing whatever was needed for their recovery, not just the procedure.

It may seem obvious that someone working in an emergency room would listen when a patient spoke about their injury or illness, but it isn't as common as you might think. Anyone who has been in a job for a length of time has heard it all. Call a computer help line and you can hear in the person's voice that they have heard your problem a hundred times that day. In the ER you have to tune out a certain amount of the suffering you see, otherwise you just couldn't handle it. ER doctors and nurses don't necessarily become numb to the pain of those around them, but they must control their emotions in order to do the best they can for the patients. Dave's message to me was a reminder that I could control my emotional response to trauma, but my duty to the patient meant that I shouldn't become unreachable.

Connecting with the customer, or the patient, takes very little extra time. Studies have shown that doctors who spend just a few minutes more per patient see a dramatic drop in malpractice law suits. In one study, vocal tracking devices were placed in examination rooms. These devices did not record conversations, for obvious legal and ethical reasons; instead they recorded the vocal pattern of the physicians. Each case was then followed to its conclusion. Those cases in which a malpractice suit was later filed the physician spoke a flat and unemotional vocal pattern. The doctors whose vocal patterns were more varied, and demonstrated an empathetic vocal pattern (remember, this is the sound of the voice, not the words themselves), were sued far less. This was true even in cases where the medical outcome was the same. Essentially, patients didn't sue doctors because a medical mistake was made, they sued doctors because they didn't like them. In some cases, when the patient was informed that the specialist whom they wished to sue was not at fault; that the fault was traced to a mistake their family doctor made, the patients said they didn't want to sue their own doctor. They still wanted to sue the specialist. Imagine how much less stress there would be for doctors, patients, and lawyers if health examinations were focused less on a list of symptoms and more on connecting with the patient.

No matter how mundane the task, there must be an important reason the job exists; and the reason must extend beyond the job description. This is the only way to create an experience the customer will appreciate, as well as a job that the employee will value. No one values a job description, they value being needed; being a part of something bigger than themselves. And if you think that some positions in a company are too task-oriented—too common—to warrant a lofty vision, guess again. The more mundane the job, the more essential it is to connect that job to a higher purpose. Feeling connected to something greater than one's self is what gives religion its power to influence millions of people; it is what creates lifelong bonds between men and women who serve in the military, and it causes people to give up valuable free time to volunteer for worthy causes. It can certainly transform your workplace.

Take a page from what we did with the housekeeping staff at the Mall of America. You can't get any more mundane and task-oriented than pushing a cleaning cart, sweeping up trash, and cleaning restrooms. When I was asked to conduct the Three Big Words program for the mall staff, I spent some time walking around the mall to get a feel for the staff (I wasn't shopping, I was *researching*, really). Whenever a member of the housekeeping staff passed by they looked like they were on their way to a funeral. Their gaze was directed to the floor and their expressions were lifeless.

I learned later why the housekeepers had such blank expressions, they were calculating; calculating how long it would take to get one task done so they could handle another. The Mall of America gets over 43 million visitors a year. Keeping a massive facility like the MOA spotless not only takes hard work, it takes a coordination of duties that would challenge a NASA flight director. Needless to say, the housekeepers had a full checklist to get through during their shift. The trouble is their facial expressions didn't look like they were thinking about their next task, they looked angry. Look at someone who is deep in thought and it is easy to mistake concentration for dissatisfaction. The other problem was the housekeepers didn't feel a connection to the mall itself. It was just a big space to keep clean. The first issue created a bad experience for the guest (no one wants to shop and play in a place where the staff looks angry), the second issue created a bad experience for the employee (no one is loyal to a cleaning cart). We had to refocus the one reason the housekeeping staff at the MOA existed.

This process wasn't just for the benefit of the housekeeping staff; maintenance, security, ride operators, movie theatre ushers, and customer service staff all deserved to feel connected to the same goal. It took weeks of discussion among the directors to finally hit on the perfect reason the MOA existed. Those two points are important: it took a long time and it was decided by leadership. Determining the one reason an organization exists should include input from as many sources as possible—employees, leaders, and customers—but the final decision must be made by leadership. Don't try to get consensus; complete agreement might be nice to have, but it is a rarity. Consensus isn't even that important; employees are willing to accept decisions from leadership as long as the staff feels like they have been heard. Time is also important. While strategies change over the years, the one reason you exist should remain for the life of the company. This is an important step in the Three Big Words process; don't rush it. If you are like most companies, after weeks of discussion and debate, you will arrive at an answer that you probably knew all along. The biggest challenge will come if two or three top executives cannot come to an agreement.

Remember the Anoka County librarians from page 26? When we talked about the one reason they existed, there was some debate. If you recall the five brand emotions—Trustworthy, Competent, Sophisticated, Rugged, or Excitement—the librarians felt that their image was probably a mix of competent and trustworthy. None of the brand emotions are better than the others, but you still have to decide once and for all which best represents your organization. If yu examine the emotion of competent, the internet is not just more convenient, it is more exciting. Playing on the internet feels just like that, playing. Going to the library feels like work. A librarian may indeed be competent, however, to a customer competence is necessary, but not desirable. In the case of librarians, competence loses out to excitement. Excitement doesn't win everywhere. We certainly don't want a surgeon who is exciting. Above all else, we want the guy with the scalpel to be competent. We will even accept a surgeon who is boring, as long as he knows what he is doing. (Of course, given the choice between a competent doctor with a great personality and one who is competent and dull, "Mr. Personality" gets the job.)

As we discussed the issue of brand emotion at the librarian's conference, one librarian said, "Look, I understand. If we were a radio station we would be National Public Radio. The internet is more like an FM rock station. But what can we do? We are NPR, not a rock station. And in the end, I would rather be NPR." This is why creating the one reason you exist is a difficult task. You cannot confuse your staff or your customers by trying to be all things to all people. The one reason you exist must fit neatly into one of the five brand emotions. In the end, the librarians decided that, while their brand emotion was competence, they still needed to attract more people to the library. And that meant having personality behind the competence.

So what are some good reasons to exist? The Mall of America chose *Make someone happy today.* Now every prospective employee is hired, not only based on their job skills, but their ability to make people happy. After all, what good is having a top-notch security force if they frighten the guests in the process? Any store can sell you stuff, but do they make you happy while doing so? A housekeeper is certainly tasked with keeping the mall spotless, but he or she is now also responsible for making sure guests have a smile on their face.

The Historic Theatre Group decided that their reason to exist was *We bring the wow.* Any theatre can sell you a ticket, show you to your seat, and entertain you, but the four venues operated by the Historic Theatre Group—the State Theatre, the Orpheum Theatre, the Pantages Theatre, and the Century Theatre—are also known for their elegance. If you are looking for a casual night of entertainment, there are plenty of options, but the Historic Theatre Group venues are for dressing up for a fancy night on the town. Now, rather than an usher simply showing you to your seat, if she notices you admiring a piece of artwork in the lobby or a chandelier in the theatre she will tell you about the artist who created it, or how the theatre found the item in an old building and transported in to their theatre. Now, when box office staff serve guests on the phone, they seek to *bring the wow* so the experience goes beyond the typical transaction.

A large hospital in Minneapolis is known for its comprehensive care, but it needed to further distinguish itself from other hospitals. Since this facility is a go-to choice for physicians who have difficult cases, the one reason they exist became *We handle the tough stuff.* An example from my own company is our *School of Improv.* Most improv companies follow a simple formula; perform comedy improv shows, and offer improv classes on the side for people interested in getting on stage. Classes provide a secondary revenue stream as well as fresh new talent.

When my business partner, Pamela Mayne, and I started Stevie Ray's Improv Company we wanted to take a different route. We knew we would have a performance troupe, but we also saw improvisation as a valuable skill for everyday life. The same techniques used to learn improvisation can improve communication skills, self-confidence, presentation skills, and teamwork. Also, we knew that the world was filled with people who had no outlet for their talents. Traditional theatre classes are not for everyone, and some of the skills taught for traditional theatre don't transfer to use at work or home. So, we made a bold decision. We marketed our improv classes solely to the non-performing artist. This was a risk because in 1989 few people were familiar with improvisation, and those that did know about it were typically actors. It took a while to gain traction, but soon "regular" people started showing up for classes. We would get a few actors or comedians here and there, but the mainstay of our school were people who wanted to learn new skills but were not interested in giving up their day jobs to pursue a career in the arts. Since then, improv training has become widely recognized as a valuable tool for personal and professional growth. We weren't the first to take this approach to improvisation training, but we were the first in our market to do so, and the distinction served us well.

Our focus on non-performing artists meant we had to pay less attention on how improv is usually taught and more on why the student was taking the class. Whereas a typical improv class would focus on acting, stage-craft, character development, and scene-work; most of our students had no interest in getting in front of the footlights. Given this, Pamela and I realized the one reason the school existed was *Helping you reach your next stage.* Having this as the focus of the classes helps remind our instructors that they are not there to teach improvisation, they are there to help each student achieve his or her individual goals.

Helping you reach your next stage may sound like an advertising slogan, and it could certainly be used as one, but the one reason your organization exists may never be displayed for public view. In fact, *Make someone happy today*, *We bring the wow*, and *We handle the tough stuff* are not part of their respective organization's marketing plans. They are internal philosophies meant to focus the employee's attention on what is truly important. For this reason, the wording must be chosen carefully. The statement must elicit an emotional response. This is why the organization's mission statement rarely fits the bill. Mission statements are often too technical and lack the emotional content needed to inspire people. This is not to say the mission statement isn't valuable. Its function is as a guide for the future of the organization, so the tenets of a mission statement should be followed by every employee.

In a workshop for a government organization, I had members of several departments in the room. This meant that each department could have a reason to exist that fit under the main reason that all government exists, *Serve the public*, but each department could have a more specific reason to exist. The workshop had staff from public health, transportation, housing, and food assistance. I had them gather in groups by department and asked them to agree on one reason their department existed. When I asked for their answers, it took some time to steer responses away from statements that sounded technical or "governmenty." One of the employees from the food assistance department responded with, "To provide residents with the necessary nutrition to ensure…" I cut her off mid-sentence (I know, that was rude of me).

I said, "Words like 'provide,' 'ensure,' 'residents,' and 'necessary' are not emotional. They also aren't the kind of words used in everyday conversation. The one reason you exist must be simple to state, easy to understand, easy to remember, and it must *feel* like something important." At that point, all the employees in that group turned to Wanda. Apparently she had suggested something to the group during their discussion that had been dismissed. Now, after I had critiqued the technical-sounding statement, her idea must have looked better. "Wanda," I said, "what is the one reason that the food assistance department exists?" She smiled and said, "We feed the babies!" Everyone in the room gasped (even the highway engineers). It doesn't get any better than that. When the right statement comes along, the whole room feels it. From now on, if there is a debate among the food assistance employees over which direction to take or which idea to accept, they have only to ask themselves "Does this idea feed the babies?" The one reason your organization exists is important because it not only identifies who you are, but who you aren't. Knowing who and what you are gives you direction, knowing what you are not eases stress.

Let's use the School of Improv as an example. Large improv organizations—The Second City in Chicago, The Groundlings in Los Angeles, or The Brave New Workshop in Minneapolis—market themselves as "star makers." The Second City performs sketch comedy similar to what you see on the TV show, *Saturday Night Live*. In fact, *Saturday Night Live* casts their actors almost exclusively from The Second City. The foundation of the theatre, however, is improvisation. Students in The Second City's improv training program walk down halls adorned with photos of the likes of John Belushi, Gilda Radner, and Bill Murray.

In Minneapolis, the Brave New Workshop was founded by Dudley Riggs, a former circus performer and vaudevillian, in

1958 (there is an ongoing battle between The Second City and the BNW as to which theatre opened first). Similar to The Second City, the Brave New Workshop performs scripted sketches developed using improvisation. Students at the BNW Student Union are surrounded by photos of Louie Anderson, Pat Proft, and Al Franken (who was a comedy writer and performer before becoming a United States Senator).

When Stevie Ray's Improv Company designed its first website, we thought it was only logical to follow the lead of these other improv companies and list the accomplishments of our alumni. Because we focus more on teaching the non-performing artist, however, we didn't have many famous faces to display, but we had a few. However, after examining the one reason we exist, we realized that *Helping you reach your next stage* had little to do with helping people become famous. Even if becoming famous is the next stage our student wants, that isn't really what we are about. We removed the alumni section from our website. It felt good to let go of the pressure of seeing how many famous careers we could launch. Rediscovering what we were not helped us focus on the needs of our students rather than our reputation.

Remember, the one reason you exist is not meant to define how you are better than other organizations, it is meant to differentiate you. It is meant to provide focus, not competition. Too many businesses compare themselves against competitors. This may have seemed like a good idea during the "Coca Cola vs. Pepsi" wars decades ago, but you might have noticed that even these two arch rivals have moved away from that strategy. The public is not only uninterested in why you think you are better than your competition, they don't trust your comparison. As soon as you start speaking in terms of better or worse, you add stress to the equation. Not only do we have to decide between the two of you, but we are worried that if we make the wrong decision we will regret it for the rest of our lives. You are better off simply telling customers exactly what to expect from you; what is the promise your company makes. Tell us why you are chicken and the other guy is fish; we'll decide which we are hungry for.

At Stevie Ray's, we discourage company members from speaking poorly about other improv companies. We rarely even use the word "competition," we like to refer to similar organizations as "colleagues" or "collaborators" in the market. We never wish ill will on our colleagues. Frankly, it is in our best interest if our colleagues do well. If one of our colleagues does poorly, it is likely because they are providing a poor product. Customers usually assume the product itself is bad, not just the company that served it. If a guest sees an improv show for the first time and it is not a good show, he or she will think all improv is bad. Instead of seeing improv at a different theatre, he will avoid it altogether. If one improv company goes down, it will take the rest with it.

Avoiding thoughts and words like "better" or "worse" takes discipline and leadership. Indeed, part of the charm of being in a club is knowing that not everyone is allowed in; this type of territorialism is hard-wired into the human brain. But the "No Girls Allowed" sign on the clubhouse door need not mean that girls are bad, they just aren't a good fit for the club. I learned the value of collaboration from colleagues at the National Speakers Association. The NSA has a strong policy of ethical behavior, and this extends to members offering testimonials for each other. Keep in mind, professional speakers are all solo entrepreneurs trying to get booked, often from the same customer.

The NSA was founded in 1973 by Cavett Robert. At the time, speakers around the country were all fighting against each other to get speaking engagements. Robert invited a bunch of speakers and introduced a novel idea, "Instead of us all fighting for our own piece of the pie, let's fight together to make the pie bigger." People told him he was crazy, that people who were all courting the same customers would never collaborate. Those naysayers were wrong. The NSA has grown to include thousands of members nationwide and has spawned the international organization, the Global Speakers Federation.

I was speaking to a client one day about possibly delivering a keynote address at her conference. At the end of the phone call she said, "We have a number of speakers to consider, but I have to tell you, when I was talking with another speaker and mentioned you were in consideration, he said, 'You can't do better than Stevie Ray! If you choose me, I will do a terrific job, but if you choose Stevie Ray I can guarantee you won't be disappointed either.' His willingness to endorse a competitor made me trust him all the more." The other speaker did differentiate himself by discussing his unique approach. He didn't position himself as better than me, just different. The client was left to make up her mind based on her needs. She ended up using the other speaker because his topic was a better fit for the theme of the conference. The following year they hired me.

I was given a reminder of the importance of respecting your colleagues during an interaction with another client years later. I was called by Gary, a member of a committee working on a conference for a major banking institution. At the end of the call he said, "It is down to you and one other speaker." He gave me the name of the speaker, which is unusual, and said he would call back in a few days to let me know the committee's decision. A few days later Gary called and said, "We're going with you." He followed with, "We at Big Ol' Bank like to give feedback to our vendors whenever we can. Would you like to know why we chose you?" Are you kidding? This kind of feedback is invaluable. He told me about the committee's decision-making process and how I was a better fit for the event. I thought that was the end of it.

Two weeks later, when I met the entire committee to go over the event, Gary pulled me aside and said, "Remember when I said that our company likes to offer helpful feedback whenever we can? Would you like to hear what the other speaker's office manager said when I told him we were going with you?" I nodded. Gary said, "As soon as I said we had chosen you, the manager said, 'Stevie Ray? We never lose business to Stevie Ray! We work with larger organizations than he does, with higher level executives, and have more business experience.'" Gary got a sly smile on his face and continued, "I stopped that little punk mid-rant and said, 'We at Big Ol' Bank have a philosophy to never speak poorly of our competition. We see them as valued colleagues to be respected. And we do not appreciate it when our vendors disrespect their competition.' That young man tried to back-peddle like you wouldn't believe. 'Oh, I didn't mean that Stevie Ray isn't good at what he does. I'm sure he is…' But I told him it was too late. Not only did he blow this job, but he shouldn't expect a call from us in the future." If you think the one reason you exist makes you better than other companies, not only are you wrong, but you could be creating a bad image in the minds of your customers.

Before reading any further, decide on the one reason you exist. Share it with employees as well as customers to see if they agree. You will probably have to make some adjustments. While you're at it, it is a cool exercise to do for your personal life as well. You can take an exercise from, *What Color Is Your Parachute?*, a classic book designed to help people determine their path in life. If you are ever in doubt as to your purpose in life, the book suggests that you imagine a party is taking place somewhere and you are not in attendance. If your name were to come up in conversation, what would you want people to say about you behind your back? Answer that question about yourself, and your business, and you have gone a long way to finding the one reason you exist.

Define:
The Three Big Words

Three Big Words
Engaged Employees • Loyal Customers

STEP ONE
Focus
Why do you exist?

STEP TWO
Define
The Three Big Words

Finally, the chapter that gave this book its title. This chapter helps you to determine if your staff is actually delivering on the promise of your one reason to exist. The reason the Three Big Words is c crucial part of the process is because it provides something most organizations lack—simplicity. The one reason you exist will provide clarity, but without the Three Big Words, the one reason can cause more frustration than direction. Take the Mall of America's *Make someone happy today*; this may seem like an initiative that would bring a smile to every employee's face. After all, who wouldn't want to focus on happiness at work all day? The problem is that employees may worry "How exactly am I supposed to make people happy?" And managers simply can't walk up to an employee at the end of a shift and ask, "Did you make someone happy today?" Most employees would respond, "I think so," or "The customer seemed satisfied."

Satisfied and *happy* are two different emotions. How is an employee supposed to know the difference? And what do you do if your employee thinks she made someone happy, but you don't? That is where the Three Big Words comes in. The Three Big Words are meant to easily define what makes a successful experience for your guest. Stevie Ray's Improv Company first developed the Three Big Words approach to solve a problem in our own company.

Ever since Stevie Ray's Improv Company began offering classes to the public in 1989, we had approximately 100 students per week. We always got enough new enrollees to make up for attrition. We were satisfied because we didn't want to have more than 100 students. However, anyone who has run a business knows that a long steady stream of business can lead to complacency. Sure enough, after about fifteen years of steady numbers we started to see a decline. We went from 100 students to 80, then to 55, then to 30. Pamela Mayne and I didn't just sit around while this was happening, we were scrambling to find the cause of the decline.

The first step was to determine where the ship was leaking. We made the same mistake a lot of companies make by looking at external factors first. Were we offering classes on days and times that the public was interested and able to attend? Was our pricing appropriate for what we were offering? After much discussion, we realized we were complicating the issue too much. A school has the same components as any business: enrollment and retention. Every business survives on how well it can attract customers (enrollment) and keep them coming back (retention). If we started with a look at those two elements, we could narrow down the problem. As we examined our statistics, we realized that our enrollment was the same as when the school was strong.

This was a relief and a frustration at the same time. It proved that our marketing was good but our delivery wasn't. And improv classes are not easy to market. Courses in things like tennis, golf, or cooking are easier to sell because everyone knows what they are. There is less hesitance in trying those kinds of classes because they teach concrete skills with a step-by-step method of learning. Improvisation is a different animal altogether. Not many people really know what it is, and there isn't as easy a method of learning. More importantly, if you don't do well at improv, the entire class sees you fail. We create a highly supportive team atmosphere, but if a student tries something during class and it bombs, no amount of teamwork can ease the sting of failure.

Another factor also affects people's willingness to take an improv class. People will often watch an entertainer—a stand-up comedian, an improv performer, or a comedy sketch actor—and think, "I could do that." However, it is safe to watch a comedy show and think, "I'm just as funny as that guy." It is a risky proposition to actually try it. If you try it an fail, it can feel worse than not having tried at all. Many dreams of greatness have remained just that; dreams. As a result, it can take people a long time to work up the courage to join one of our classes. We have been told by students that they were on our e-mail list for 2-3 years before finally gathering up the nerve to join.

With all that stress behind the simple decision to join our classes, you can see why we were so upset when people would leave after only a few months. In the early days our students would stay in classes for an average of one year; some students stayed for over ten years. Having students quit after two or three months was unacceptable, and it pointed to something far more complicated than the class schedule or the price; we were not delivering on our promise. So we had some long conversations with our instructors. When we asked them if the classes felt successful to them they said, "We're teaching the same curriculum as always," and "My students seem to like the class." We knew that even though this is what we wanted to hear, something was missing in the way we trained our instructors to deliver a great experience. That is when we hit on the idea of the Three Big Words.

Actually, we were guided to the Three Big Words by some wise mentors. One was Gary Jader, a member of our board of directors and a marketing expert. While Gary was on the board he reminded us that *it's not what you do, it's what you get done that matters*. He said, "This may be hard to accept because you have devoted so much of your career to learning and teaching improvisation, but nobody cares about improv. Besides the fact that few people actually know what it is, they don't care about improvisation per se. What they care about is what improv can do for them. They don't want to learn improv, they want to learn to think quicker, be more confident, or speak better. Don't focus on teaching improv, focus on what it can do for people." When we thought about Gary's advice we realized that the instructors' focusing on the curriculum was keeping them from focusing on the students.

Since Pamela was in charge of the School of Improv, she and the instructors took a few weeks to answer the question,

"Which three words define a successful experience for our students?" We would determine three specific words that, if in place, meant that every student was getting the exact experience we wanted them to have. Those three words would be used a measuring stick to define a successful improv class for every student, no matter what their reasons were for attending. By creating a three-word standard we would eliminate any guess work. Instead of asking an instructor if he or she "ran a good class" or "gave the students a good experience," we would simply ask if they kept the three-word standard in place.

It took a couple of weeks for them to agree on the right combination of words, but she finally called and said, "We have it! Every class needs to be *safe, fun,* and *challenging*." We talked about how they chose safe, fun, and challenging as the measure of a successful improv class. *Safe* was the first word because it can be the most difficult quality to maintain; given that most of the students were trying something completely foreign to them. Every student deserved a safe environment in which to experiment and learn new skills. *Fun* is important because, no matter how important an endeavor is, it if isn't fun we will find excuses to avoid doing it. *Challenging* spoke to the responsibility of each instructor to focus on the student's reason for being in class. If one student was there to improve professional skills and another student wanted more self-confidence in social situations, they both needed to be challenged in ways that respected their goals.

Once we had the Three Big Words for the school in place, our conversations with instructors and students changed dramatically. We began to focus less on the curriculum and more on why we placed certain exercises on certain days. There needed to be a reason for our decisions that satisfied the Three Big Words as well as the one reason the school existed. We asked instructors questions like, "What did you do to make the students feel safe?" If the instructor responded with, "The students seemed to feel comfortable" that wasn't a good enough answer. We need to know that the instructors were taking conscious steps to make every student feel safe, have fun, and be challenged. With the Three Big Words as a guide, nothing would be left to chance. With all the work it takes to market the classes and attract customers, the only way to serve the student and improve retention was to clearly define what a successful class looked like.

Many companies focus on how well they perform their duties or tasks and assume that if they perform satisfactorily the customer will return. This is the thinking I mentioned earlier, the belief that customer service is the reason customers return; satisfactory service is not the same as memorable service. Most companies track things like speed of service and number of customer complaints. They believe that if there are no complaints everyone must be happy. No news is good news. This approach misses the bigger picture.

The Three Big Words not only changed how we taught our classes, it changed how we identified success. Earlier I wrote about how most improv companies define success by how many students go on to "make it big." When we decided that the mark of success for us were classes that were safe, fun, and challenging, we changed how we viewed our outcomes. We no longer cared if one of our students became famous, we paid more attention to the everyday student who accomplished his or her personal goals. Now, when people ask, "Do you have any success stories of students who took your improv classes?" we know what they mean (anyone famous?), but we answer with how we define success.

A great example is Curt. Curt was a young man in his mid-twenties. He was diagnosed clinically agoraphobic; an anxiety disorder usually brought on by open spaces or crowded environments. For a person with agoraphobia a shopping mall would be the most frightening place to be. Curt's condition was so severe that the thought of going out of his house left him paralyzed with fear. He lived on disability payments and rarely left home. His therapist suggested our classes as a way to build confidence in a safe, controlled environment. Curt happened to join a class taught by Pamela. Because of our new-found focus on student experience instead of strict adherence to a curriculum, Pamela taught him quite differently than the other students in his class. As you might guess, the element of safety would be a primary concern for someone suffering from agoraphobia. Pamela addressed this by privately telling Curt that during every class he would sit in the chair next to Pamela. She referred to this as his *safe spot*. The rest of the students were not told of this; Pamela simply placed her teacher's manual on that chair whenever Curt was not seated, and remove it when it was his turn to sit.

By creating a safe spot for Curt, Pamela would become a steadfast, familiar element in an otherwise free-wheeling environment. She would also quietly give Curt directions during class. She knew she still needed to challenge Curt, but the challenge needed to be specific to his needs. So, while the rest of the class might be working on physicality or building upon each other's ideas, Pamela would whisper to Curt that his goal would be to look three people in the eye during the next exercise—agoraphobics often have difficulty making eye contact. This simple goal was part of a step-by-step system Pamela created to bring Curt out of himself.

With safety fully in place, it was easier to make the class fun for Curt, which happened every time he said something funny during an exercise and was rewarded with the laughter of his classmates. And laugh they did. We discovered something about Curt that most of the world didn't know; he was funny. He possessed a remarkable sense of humor and a keen wit. He brought ideas to improv that were creative as well as funny. All this talent was hidden from the world because he couldn't leave his house. A class that was safe, fun, and challenging allowed it to shine. The compliments he received from Pamela and his classmates were like gold. He learned that he had something valuable to offer the world.

For many years, Stevie Ray's Improv Company would offer outdoor *Improv in the Park* shows to the public. We would combine professional troupe members with students from the school for each show so students could have their first opportunity to perform for a live audience. Having professionals to lend support gave the newcomers confidence to try the scariest challenge anyone could face; performing comedy in front of strangers. If you think giving a speech at work will make your knees shake, try performing comedy in front of an expecting audience. After only a year and a half of classed, Curt performed improv in front of a crowd of 300 people at an Improv in the Park show. Years later he married a fellow improv student, had secured a regular job, and was still as funny as ever.

I don't tell you the story of Curt to promise that the Three Big Words will turn your life around, or the lives of your employees, customers, or guests, but it might. If it isn't a life-changer, it can make work easier by knowing exactly what to look for in every interaction between the people you work with and the people you serve. At the very least it reduces stress by replacing vague goals with concrete language. Every type of company can define a successful experience with Three Big Words. And resist the temptation to have more than three words. Remember from earlier in the book, we brain remembers everything better in groups of three.

Let's look at examples of other three-word combinations and why they are so specific. When we hire performers for Stevie

Ray's Comedy Cabaret we teach them the three words that define a successful show; Fun, Funny, and Professional. There are many different styles of comedy. Some will make you laugh, but in a mean-spirited way. We don't look down upon these styles of shows or the performers that offer them, we just don't offer that style at our cabaret. In order for a show to be successful, the audience must leave feeling uplifted. They must have had a *fun* night. Also, some forms of entertainment are interesting, but not necessarily funny. The sign on our door reads Stevie Ray's *Comedy* Cabaret, so the promise is that you will laugh. We tell members of *The Stevie Ray's Comedy Troupe* that if the audience isn't holding their sides with laughter, it isn't a successful show.

The third quality—Professional—grew out of a need to differentiate our service from the rest of the market. A large number of improv troupes in the country approach performance with a more casual attitude, which is reflected in their wardrobe and performance style. Some of them take to the stage looking like they pulled their clothes out of the dirty laundry hamper. This is not at all meant as a criticism of these performers. They have identified their market and serve them well. Our audiences expect a certain approach that is less casual, so chose Professional as one of our Three Big Words to remind our performers that we want our audiences to be as impressed with us as they are entertained. A show that is fun, funny, and professional defines a successful experience at any of our shows.

To respect the privacy of our clients, I won't share with you their Three Big Words, but I will offer some thoughts as you think of your own. Like the other elements discussed thus far, the Three Big Words must strike an emotional chord; both for the employee—who must feel passionately about his or her work—and for the customer who will be the recipient of your service. Avoid the temptation to use trendy words like *empower* or *engage*. It is rare that you hear those words in everyday conversation. The Three Big Words you choose will guide your staff every day; words that sound too technical may serve the ego, but they don't motivate. Remember what our friend Gary Jader said, this is not about what you do, it is about what you get done for others.

Emotional Words	**Technical Words**
Happy	Satisfied
Play	Engaged
Considerate	Focused
Warm	Purposeful
Friendly	Driven
Concerned	Aligned
Tenacious	Centered
Content	Competent
Quiet	Excellence
Peaceful	Oriented
Thrilled	Outcome
Enthusiastic	Positive
Connected	Successful

Remember the advice about Brand Emotions from the past chapter? The Three Big Words are where your Brand Emotion is brought to life. If you look at the lists above you will *feel* something when you read the emotional words; you will *think* something with the technical words. Think only of what would define a successful experience for your customers. If you can get to the heart of a successful guest experience, you will create the kind of atmosphere that is also great for your employees.

When I was conducting a workshop for university professors I asked them to decide the Three Big Words that would define a successful class. Those who had their focus where it belonged—on the student—used words like excitement, curiosity, laughter, enlightened, and bonding. One professor said one of her words would have to be *neuroscience-based*. How much fun do you think that class would be? When I asked about her choice she said that too many courses taught elsewhere were worthless because they weren't based on current research. She wanted people to know that her course was valid. This professor is a good example of what can happen if you think of yourself instead of the customer. She didn't decide on *neuroscience-based* because the students wanted it, she chose it to take a stab at other professors she thought were inadequate. The student doesn't appear anywhere in her thinking. Trying to prove that you are better than the competition is a wasted effort. First, we won't believe you even if you are better. Second, you aren't.

Don't get me wrong, I am a big follower of neuroscience, but including current research in a class isn't an extra–it is expected. Expecting praise because your facts are accurate is like telling people on a cruise that you made sure there were no holes in the ship. Be sure to examine all options before deciding your Three Big Words. Not only do they need to carry an emotional punch, they need to be dead-on accurate for your business. For instance, at one company we debated for an entire meeting over *friendly* versus *welcoming*. This may seem trivial, but if three words are going to define your company for years to come you had better get it right the first time. Also, there is a big difference on how your staff will interpret one word over another. For instance, friendly means that someone is pleasant to others. Welcoming, however, means that the employee will take the extra step of engaging with the other person. Friendly will smile back when you say hello, welcoming will meet you at the door. Simple distinctions have important implications for how your employees will view their role in the organization.

Just having the Three Big Words is not, however, enough to engage employees and create loyal customers. In fact, without the next step, the Three Big Words are dangerous. Imagine a manager asking an employee, "Were you welcoming today?" One person's welcoming is another person's stalking. Not only do people have different interpretations of words, few people can objectively review their own performance. You need to add the next step to simplify the process and make expectations easy to understand and put into practice. That next step involves giving employees actionable steps they can take to ensure they are putting the Three Big Words into practice every day.

Implement:
Simple Acts

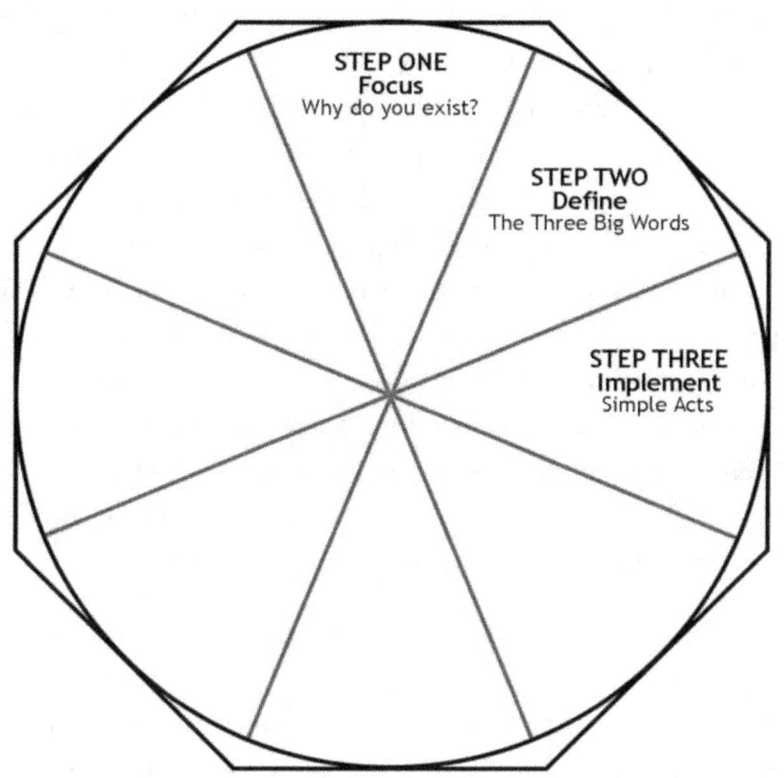

I guess I lied in the last chapter when I said I would keep my clients' Three Big Words private. In order to explain Simple Acts I need to show how they are put in motion. And the Simple Acts are tied directly to the Three Big Words, so... One of the Three Big Words at the Mall of America was *Friendly*. (You guessed it. That was the debate I spoke of about the difference between Friendly and Welcoming.) The reason Friendly was considered an important Big Word is that the Mall of America, being roughly the size of Montana, can seem like an unfriendly place. The simple fact that so many people occupy the same place at the same time can be scary. The paradox is that, while visitors are attracted to the Mall of America because it is the most popular tourist destination in the country, they seem surprised that so many other people are there, too. I was showing a friend around the MOA for the first time and he asked, "Where did all these people come from?" I replied, "They are wondering the same thing about you."

Another paradox is that the MOA is located in Minnesota, where the people have long been known for being *Minnesota Nice*. People new to Minnesota often joke about having to wait forever at a four-way intersection because everyone is trying to let the other drivers go first. So, for the MOA to seem unfriendly goes against the grain of Minnesota culture (most locals assume any rudeness must be from a tourist). One way that any large venue can seem unfriendly is when a guest can't find what he or she is looking for. And having to search for help causes stress, the opposite of the experience the mall is trying to create. Think back to the last time you went to buy a new stopper-thingy for your toilet at a big-box home improvement store. After wandering the aisles looking for the plumbing department, then finding the plumbing area but not seeing toilet stoppers, did you finally ask yourself, "Does anybody actually work here?"

The folks at the MOA were not blind to the challenge of creating a friendly atmosphere with the obstacle of serving millions of people in a huge venue. The problem was that employees were either focused solely on their own jobs, or didn't know exactly how the mall directors defined friendly. The first issue, employees being focused only on their jobs, is common in most companies. Housekeepers were focused on cleaning, maintenance crews were focused on running from broken thing to broken thing and fixing them. Security was focused on keeping everyone safe. The only people actually charged with being friendly were the guest services employees. These employees were stationed at service desks at the various entrances to the mall; another challenge because few people need help when they are either entering or leaving the building. Our first task was to get every employee to understand that they had a role in making the Mall of America a friendly place.

The leadership at the MOA wisely decided to have me work first with the housekeeping employees. This was a good decision because housekeeping represented not only one of the largest employee groups in the mall, but the staff was the most visible. If guests were going to feel like the MOA was a friendly place, the housekeeping crew needed to be fully on board. At each meeting with housekeeping crews, we first introduced the One Reason the Mall of America exists, then explained the Three Big Words. By then, we knew that employees would be nervous. They would likely be thinking "How am I supposed to be all those things while still trying to do my job?" This is when the Simple Acts are introduced; they provide the calm of simplicity and the confidence to meet the challenge.

For each group, I promised the employees I would be completely honest with them and expected their honest input in return. I said that, in preparation for my work with them, I spent a lot of time at the mall observing the guests and the staff. I said that I saw a pretty consistent picture from day to day. I asked the housekeepers, "How many of you see this face every day?" I took on the expression of a guest who was completely lost and confused. Of course, all the employees raised their hands. Then I followed with, "Here is where I promised to be honest with you. The saddest thing for me was to see guests who looked completely lost, but seeing you folks walk right by them without offering to help."

I asked the housekeepers, "Whose job is it to help the guest? To make the guest feel welcome?" The typical response was, "Guest Services." I would then ask, "Where is Guest Services?" "At the mall entrance," they would reply. I would say, "So you're telling me that a guest standing in the middle of the amusement park, or the food court, or an atrium is supposed to walk two and a half miles to an entrance to get the help you—standing right next to them—could provide instantly?"

I never actually heard the phrase "But that's not my job" or "That's not what I was hired to do" from any of the mall employees, but you can be sure that thought floated through a few heads. There is a risk of any employee having those thoughts, unless they are trained not to. When working with the housekeeping staff we discovered that the only thing holding them back from interacting with guests was that they didn't know they had permission to do so. Many of them said they thought they would get in trouble if they spoke to people. They thought that managers would assume they were slacking off and not attending to their housekeeping duties. So part of the training had to include the message that the guests were the highest priority; even though the housekeepers would be expected to keep the place clean, they could still make guests feel like the MOA was a friendly place while doing so. The housekeeping staff needed what every employee needs—permission accompanied by expectation.

Now that the staff knew they had permission, as well as the expectation, to be the friendly face of the Mall of America, we needed to spell out exactly what that would look like. You can't just ask an employee at the end of the day, "Were you friendly?" People have different interpretations of what friendly looks like. The MOA needed to tell employees what it means to be friendly at the Mall of America. And the staff needed to know just how they would be evaluated and rewarded in doing so. That is where the Simple Acts comes in.

Each of your Three Big Words will have three Simple Acts that every employee is expected to perform every day; a total of nine simple acts that should become part of every work day. The housekeepers were told the three simple acts that supported a friendly mall:

1) Look up, not down. When guests walk by, make eye contact.

2) When you make eye contact, smile.

3) If you see a guest who looks lost or confused, approach them and say, "Hi. My name is _____. I work here at the mall. You look a little lost. I know where everything is. What can I help you find?"

These Simple Acts might seem beyond simple; they might seem ridiculously simple. That is true. The reason they are called Simple Acts is that they must be so clear that there is no room for interpretation. Asking someone "Were you friendly today?" is asking for their interpretation of friendly. What do you do if an employee thinks walking by a lost guest is still friendly, as long as they smiled at the guest? You can't go around firing everyone who thinks of friendly differently than you; hoping to eventually hire all like-minded people. You can, however, easily ask, "How many people did you smile at today?" or "How many people did you offer to help today?"

Simple Acts only count if they can be counted. You can't actually count how many times you were friendly in a day, but you can count how many times you smiled. Being able to count the act removes doubt and confusion. Simple Acts must also be reasonable. How easy is it for a housekeeper pushing a cleaning cart to simply look up instead of down? How easy is it for a manager to remind someone to smile? Simple Acts make life easier for managers and employees alike. Without the risk of subjectivity, everyone knows by what yardstick they will be measured. Here are some Simple Acts that try to accomplish the same goal, but either hit or miss the mark:

Good
Shake each guest's hand.
Not So Good
Be genuine and friendly.

Good
Assure the guest you will find the answer and call them back.
Not So Good
Simplify the process.

Good
Never make the customer call back, assure him or her that you will find the answer and call them back.

Not So Good
Simplify the process.

Good
Ask three questions about the customer's project.
Not So Good
Seek a greater understanding of the customer's needs.

As you can see, all of the above are worthy goals, the Not So Good ideas are not Simple Acts because you can't really count how many times someone was genuine. And you cannot clearly define what it means to gain a greater understanding of the customer's needs. And without absolute clarity, the employees and managers can't work together to achieve the goal. Actually, *Simplify the process* is a great goal, *Never make the customer call back* is the Simple Act to accomplish the goal.

Simple Acts must also fit within the employee's regular duties, and offer a reasonable stretch of capabilities. Obviously, looking up and smiling is a simple addition to the day's tasks and wouldn't detract from the work itself. Helping a guest get to where they're going, however, is a bit of a stretch. This would require an employee to make a judgement call based on the situation and the needs of the guest. If the situation warranted, the housekeeper may need to push his or her cleaning cart into a nearby closet and walk the guest to their destination. This type of stretch requires more than just the assurance that the employee was capable of handling the challenge, it requires the assurance that managers would not crack down on the employee for "not doing their job."

Simple Acts must also seem natural for the person being asked to do them. Smiling is only natural when it comes naturally. We have all encountered the sales person who smiles a bit too much. At that point, *friendly* is replaced by *creepy*. This is why the Simple Act only asked that housekeepers smile when they made face-to-face contact with someone; whether they are a guest or another employee.

Having employees act naturally may seem like an oversimplification, but many companies make employees act unnaturally. They are so desperate to create a good image that they go overboard with false fun. I was standing at the customer service desk of *Tire City* to have new tires installed on my car. (Who knew tires weren't supposed to last 125,000 miles?) While I was filling out the customer form with my name, address, make and model of the car, and the date of my last tetanus vaccination, the phone rang. The guy with the grungy coveralls, three-day growth of beard, and greasy fingernails snatched up the phone and said, "We're having a great day down here at Tire City. This is Ben. How can I make it a fantastic day for you?" I don't mean to sound cynical, but is anyone really having that great a day at Tire City. It certainly didn't look like Ben was having a great day at Tire City. Having to spew out that drivel every time he answered the phone wasn't making his day at Tire City any greater. I'll bet that whoever decided on that as the standard greeting for the company didn't take the time to find out if customers actually wanted to hear that when they called about getting a front-end alignment.

Some employees at the Mall of America challenged me on having Friendly as one of the Three Big Words. One employee said, "I hate it when I go into a store and the clerks fake friendliness just to sell you stuff. They hound you with questions like 'What can I help you find?' 'Are you looking for anything in particular?' 'Have you heard about our new rewards program?' I just want to be left alone to shop." I assured these employees that I shared their disdain for pushy sales people, I explained that serving the guest means paying attention to what they really want; not treating them all the same with standard greetings or sales pitches. If a guest's body language clearly signals "Leave me alone," leave them alone. Pushy is the opposite of friendly.

The Simple Acts are not meant to replace the employee's intuition; the acts are meant to enhance awareness. Many companies try to standardize every detail of the process. The assumption is that if you remove variables from the process, you will ensure a consistent product or experience. McDonald's restaurants did this when they dictated the exact thickness that each hamburger must be produced by the manufacturer. Cooks at McDonald's are trained to grill each burger for an exact number of minutes per side in order to achieve the proper temperature. Standardized processes are certainly appropriate in some situations—cooking fast-food burgers, for instance—but they don't solve every problem; and they can actually create others. When I was a teenager I was a cook at an A&W restaurant. Although there were many standardized procedures we were also trained to use our heads. I wasn't taught to place a burger on the grill and hit a timer. I was trained to look for the signs that a burger was ready to flip and when it was ready to take off the grill. I apprenticed under a more experienced cook until I proved that I was a reliable judge of my own cooking skills. This process was certainly more complicated than the McDonald's procedure, but it produced a different kind of employee. I didn't *time* things, I cooked. Being responsible for the outcome of my work made me take greater pride in my job. As a result, I was reluctant to jump ship just because another job offered a few cents more per hour.

The Simple Acts are not an out-of-the-box set of actions, but a first step toward developing the employee's skills and intuition. For more on standardization vs. intuition, read *The Design of Business* by Roger Martin, dean and professor of strategic management of the Rotman School of Management at the University of Toronto. He makes it clear when standardization is a perfect move for a company, and when intuition should be favored.

Many companies have responded to the challenge of employee engagement/customer loyalty by moving in the wrong direction. Rather than help the employees who have the most customer contact do better at connecting with the guest, they forget that certain employees are an important part of the guest's experience. When you stay at a hotel you are likely to see housekeeping and maintenance employees more than the front desk clerk, but when you pass a housekeeper in the hallway you usually only get a quick smile and nod. Front line employees have the greatest impact on how a customer feels, but are often given the fewest tools to make a positive difference. This is where the Simple Acts come in. The Simple Acts are steps that any employee can take to make a difference.

Simple Acts also solve another challenge; barriers. Front line employees often feel uncomfortable engaging with the customer; either because it isn't part of their job, or because they might feel inadequate at dealing with customers. At one hotel chain, the directors told me that some housekeepers only smile and nod at customers because the employee is new to the country and unsure of their English language skills. The Simple Acts help alleviate this stress. If the employee is given a clearly defined action to perform, this assures them that they will not be held accountable for an action that is not defined. And, just as important, the employee is given both the permission to engage and the expectation to engage. In the case of the hotel housekeepers, the managers assured them that smiling and talking to guests did not mean they would be expected to handle more complex issues if any arose. What surprised the managers was that by only requiring a few Simple Acts, the staff ended up performing services far beyond what was required of them. The simple opening of the door created a whole new level of engagement.

Focusing on Simple Acts changes a manager's approach to leading employees. Most managers waste their time micromanaging behaviors instead of tracking outcomes. They become clock-watchers instead of motivators. They assume that, if they make sure everyone gets to work on time and keeps their nose to the grindstone, productivity will follow. What these managers get for their trouble is a disengaged workforce. If your job was just like a cook at McDonald's, where all you had to do was slap a burger on the grill and hit a timer, how much would you really care about your productivity?

I was working with a large telecommunications company that was experiencing low employee morale. The division I worked with dealt with corporate customer accounts. The staff spent their days calling large clients who were delinquent in their payments and tried to get the client to submit a payment. This sometimes involved the nasty task of having to threaten to cut off phone service if a payment agreement couldn't be reached. You can imagine the panic and anger a client would feel at the prospect of having valuable phone service taken away. So the account rep would have to try to get money while managing a tense interaction with the client. Since the amount of money recovered for the company was tied to how many clients the rep called each day, the company leaders thought they could improve productivity by installing a computer system that would track the number of minutes each employee spent on the phone. Any time not spent on the phone was considered PT, "Personal time." Managers were tasked with ensuring each employee's PT stayed low. The simple assumption was that the more time employees spent on the phone, the more money the company could recover.

What the company didn't take into account was what kind of environment this would create between management and staff. The managers forgot the real reason the division existed—recovering money—and instead became clock-watchers. When I spoke with the employees I asked them what gave them the greatest satisfaction about their jobs (keep in mind these employees had to call clients who weren't too keen on getting this phone call in the first place). The employees all had the same sentiment. Although they felt good about recovering money for the company, they felt the greatest pride in helping a client get out of a jam. One employee said, "When I can call a client, I know he or she is nervous because they are behind on their bill. When I work out a payment plan so they can keep their service and take steps toward paying off their debt; I feel great. Now they don't have to be nervous about getting 'the call' from us anymore. I don't see my job as being a debt collector. I am a problem solver!"

These kinds of conversations made me feel great, then I spoke to Margie. She held the number two spot in the division; she collected more recovered money than almost everyone else in the division. When I asked her what kind of feedback she got from her manager she said, "At every employee evaluation, all he says is that my PT time is too high." The only reason the division exists is to recover money, and Margie is second best at doing just that; but rather than focus on the outcome, the manager tracks her behavior. Margie said, "These managers are so focused on our PT time I've seen one of them follow employees to the bathroom to time how long they take."

I had a workshop scheduled with the managers the following week, so I thought it was a good opportunity to address the issue. When I addressed the managers I said, "I understand that some of you might be following employees to the bathroom to track their time. You might want to reconsider whether that is creating the outcome you want." A voice from the back of the room piped up, "Well we wouldn't have to follow them if they didn't take a newspaper and sit in there for a half hour." I could see this was going to be a long meeting. "What is your job?" I asked. They replied, "To keep people productive." I asked, "What is the measure of productivity for this division?" The managers replied with a chorus of "Low PT!" I countered, "Productivity for this division is measured by one thing, and one thing only; how much money is recovered. If an employee works only two hours a day, but recovers more money than everyone else, she is not your problem. As long as she is your top producer the only thing you should be worried about is how to keep her happy. Your problem is the person who works eight hours a day, but recovers no money." You have been fooled into thinking that if you manage people's behaviors, that will lead to the best outcome. That puts you in the role of a parent, not a manager. Parents say 'Sit up straight. Eat your vegetables. No kicking each other under the table.' Employees don't come to work hoping for another set of parents to watch over. They want someone who will collaborate with them to create a successful outcome."

I told them the story of my friend Pete. Pete is a CEO of a computer storage company. One day Pete called Bart, one of his salesmen into his office and fired him. The salesman was shocked and said, "I can't believe you're firing me. I am in the office every day at least an hour before anyone else. And I stay later, too." Pete said, "You need to learn the difference between keeping busy and getting stuff done. What good is it to me to have a salesman who is busy if he doesn't sell anything? You may be here a lot, but your numbers are the worst in the office. If Jenny comes to work late and leaves early, but has the best sales in the company, I don't care what she does the rest of the time."

I told the managers something that they weren't expecting; that it was really none of their business what the staff did with their time. The only concern of theirs was the amount of money recovered. Who arrived late or left early made no difference, the only thing that mattered to the company was the desired outcome. Some managers felt that I had just taken away the only way they could justify their existence. If they didn't keep track of their employees' behavior, what use were they. So we had to replace their old-style tracking activities with actions that would truly motivate and engage their staff. They would still manage their teams, but they would motivate and coach; not parent. It is much easier to track arbitrary behaviors than it is to create paths for your staff to be successful. This is the true focus of Simple Acts; creating an environment where the actions of the staff have a direct impact on the guest's experience, and helps the employee gain a sense of success each and every day. Instead of simply keeping busy, they are getting things done.

The other great outcome of Simple Acts is that conversations between management and staff become easier, less contentious, more focused, and more cooperative. If management and staff can agree, for instance, that front line employees will engage in a simple activity, it is easy to ask if the activity was performed. At a local wireless service store, the staff will walk each customer to the door at the end of the visit, hold the door open, and say goodbye. It isn't a big deal, but it is a noticeable difference in the experience you usually get at a place like that. This Simple Act is easy for management to discuss.

"How many times did you hold a door open for a guest?"
"Fifteen times today."
"What did you notice as a result?"

The conversation is not only easy (because there is clarity of expectations), but it is cooperative. Rather than checking up on the employee, the conversation becomes one in which both parties are working to achieve the same goal. The conversation is focused on the customer experience and the employee's feelings, so there in less contention.

All this leads to the greatest advantage Simple Acts provides—experimentation. The Simple Acts you create are not static, they are a starting point. The assumption may be that making eye contact and smiling at guests will create a more comfortable environment; thereby increasing customer loyalty. But what if you are wrong? What if the statistics don't improve after a few months of eye contact and smiling? No problem. Change the Simple Acts. CEOs across America were surveyed to determine commonalities in their thinking. No matter what industry they represented, they all shared one common attitude, *I don't make mistakes. I make adjustments.* Great leaders don't dwell on why a plan didn't work. They create a new plan, a new experiment. You can create as many Simple Acts as your imagination will allow. How long you allow each Simple Act to remain in place before deciding whether is it a success depends on you and your business. Just make sure your timeline and goals are reasonable.

So how do you create an environment where you employees want to engage in the Simple Acts? First, you have to understand why they would not. Fear of failure is what keeps most people from trying new things. In the book, *Influencer: The Power to Change Anything,* authors Kerry Patterson, Joseph Grenny, David Maxfield, Ron McMillan, and Al Switzler compared how various organizations were able to successfully introduce massive culture change. They investigated how the World Health Organization was able to rid West Asian and Sub-Saharan tribal communities of the deadly Guinea worm virus and compared their methods with those of the Delancey

Street Foundation, a center in San Francisco that had a 90% success rate in helping those with drug and alcohol addiction (the national success rate is far lower). What the researchers discovered was that, whenever you ask someone to change their behavior, they ask themselves two questions: "*Should* I do it?" and "*Can* I do it?"

The *should I do it* question translates into, "What is in it for me?" Humans are wired with a strong self-interest. If there isn't a personal benefit to engaging in new behavior, it isn't worth the effort. Before you ask employees to perform the Simple Acts, you need to know what the benefit is for them. And remember, helping the company succeed isn't a benefit for the employee. It has to be much more personal. The benefit only needs to be proportional to the task being requested. If all you are asking for is a simple, friendly acknowledgement of a customer, the benefit for the employee doesn't need to be Earth-shaking. If you are asking employees to go further out of their daily routine, however, the benefit has to be bigger. In most cases, the benefit often only needs to be recognition for a job well done. Praise almost always trumps pay. (Unless you pay your staff lousy wages. If so, you have a different problem on your hands.)

The *can I do it* question relates to the chances of failure. If there is a high risk of failure, the employee will not engage in the new behavior. One of the most powerful forces affecting our decision making is how our behavior will be perceived by others. Our place in society is important. If the Simple Act you ask of your employees carries a high risk of failure, there are few benefits big enough to be worth failing in front of others. So make sure the Simple Acts you create not only carry a benefit for the employee and are such that they will be sure to be successful.

There in an understanding among managers; *you can train skills, but you can't train attitude*. As you can easily see, none of the ideas suggested so far will work if they are approached with a poor attitude. And, since you can't train attitude, let's move on to the next step; hiring people with the attitude you need.

Hire:
Who Gets In the Club House?

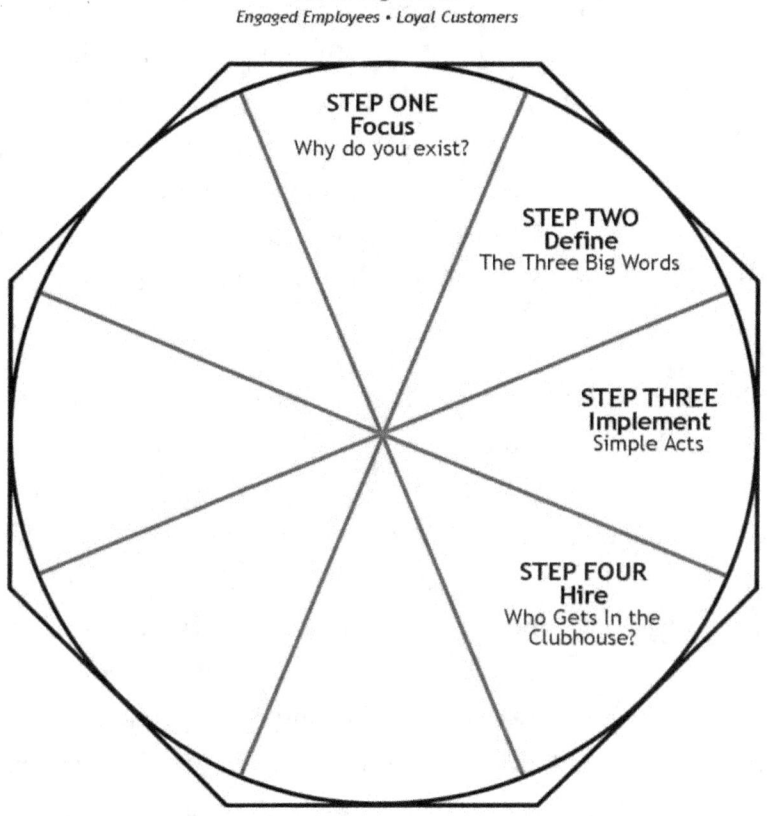

In his bestselling book, *Good to Great*, Jim Collins put forth the idea that it is less important to find people with specific abilities and more important to form the right team. Collins calls it getting "the right people on the bus." In his research into why some companies outperformed their competition, even when faced with the same challenges, Collins discovered that companies simply cannot motivate employees; employees are either self-motivated or not. No amount of training will change that. If that is the case, then more focus must be placed on the hiring process itself. Too often, hiring managers are simply told to look for candidates with the proper qualifications to perform the tasks required of them. As a result, the company only finds out that the person is a poor fit for the culture after the damage is done.

The first step to solving this dilemma is to make the One Reason You Exist, the Three Big Words, and the Simple Acts part of the interview. Imagine a guy interviewing for the job of a mechanic at a car dealership. He will expect the interview to involve the hours per week he will work, the policies of the company, and some questions about his previous experience. According to conventional wisdom, if the candidate has relevant experience and understands the policies of the company; everything will be hunky-dory. Then, a few months into his employment, you start hearing about personality clashes. Imagine if a prospective auto mechanic were told, "The one reason we exist is to make people feel *comfortable* about their cars. During every step of the process; selection, negotiating the sale, delivery, regular maintenance, and repairs, the only thing that matters is that the guest feels comfortable. Other dealers focus on the excitement of having a car, which is fine, but that isn't us. We're all about comfort. As for the job you are applying for, any dealership can fix a car, but we make people comfortable while doing it." If the prospective mechanic was a loner who didn't really feel comfortable around customers, if he would rather keep his head under the hood when the car's owner walked in, he might not be a good fit for that dealership. He might be a great mechanic, but not a great mechanic for you. Having this kind of conversation right from the start would allow him to decide for himself that he wasn't a good fit. After all, when the "No Girls Allowed" sign is put on the door to the clubhouse, most girls don't want to join that club anyway.

Also imagine if the mechanic was told, "There are three things that we consider to be crucial in making every customer comfortable. Every interaction must include Fun, Learning, and Surprise. No one thinks getting their car fixed is fun, but it actually can be if the people who work here make it fun. Years ago, no one would have dreamed that watching the safety speech from a flight attendant would be fun, but look at Southwest Airlines. If they can do it, so can we. Also, we want every employee to see coming to work here every day as fun. So the fun extends to each other, not just the guest. In addition, we think that if a car owner knows a little bit more about their car, they will feel more comfortable working with us. So we ask that each interaction involve you educating them on one small thing they might not have known. We don't want you to overload them with too much information, so we keep it to the level of their interest. And finally, if everything only goes according to plan for the customer, we don't stand out. There is nothing unique about a customer bringing their car to us, us fixing it, and them driving home. That is when we are at the greatest risk of losing our customers to another shop that might be offering a special or is open more hours than us. So we ask our employees to add one little surprise to each visit. Maybe you fixed a little something in addition to the problem they experienced. Maybe you saw a fishing rod in the back seat of the car so you tossed an issue of a fishing magazine in the front seat as a gift (we'll pay for it). But you need to be willing to be on your toes to go beyond just fixing the car, and surprise our customers. We also like to surprise each other. We throw impromptu parties, celebrate milestones in each other's lives, and generally show that we care enough about each other to do more than just work side by side. Before we continue with the interview, we need to talk about whether this kind of place is a good fit for you."

The above requirements might actually scare off a number of candidates, especially those who just want to keep their head down and do their job. That is a good thing. You don't want them as employees anyway. If they are frightened of these requirements, it is a sure bet they would be the ones resisting other changes you introduce in the future. A mechanic who understands the true nature of the job will be willing to be a partner in the success of the company, not just a wrench turner. This holds true for every employee, from the new hire to the folks in the C-Suites.

If describing the One Reason You Exist as well as the Three Big Words wasn't enough of a filter to strain out a poor-fit mechanic, the Simple Acts certainly would be. The conversation might include, "We have three easy steps to make sure Fun, Learning, and Surprise are part of every guest experience. We call them Simple Acts. For example, to make sure Learning is part of the experience one Simple Act is that we ask that whenever you return a vehicle to the owner, you explain the repairs that were made. A lot of auto shops just hand over the invoice and assume the owner will read it, but that stuff can be kind of complicated, so we prefer that one of us explain things in plain language. Another Simple Act is that you tell the owner if there is anything he or she can do to keep his or her car in good condition. For instance, if you notice uneven wear on the tires, remind them that tire rotations and wheel alignments are a lot cheaper than a new set of tires. For the third Simple Act under Learning, we send out an e-mail newsletter once a month with quick reminders about common problems car owners might face and how to solve them without running up a big bill. You would be asked to help with the newsletter by offering ideas based on interactions you have with our guests."

Including the Simple Acts is important during the hiring process. It sets up clear expectations from the start and avoids surprises later on. When kids are getting ready to play a game, the first thing they do is agree on the rules. The most important rule for most games are *the bounds*. Every player has to know that going past the telephone pole or the green car is *out of bounds*. If any player goes past the green car, the others get to call her on it. She is either *it*, or has to sit in the penalty area for a while; either way, she knew where the bounds were before the game started. Adults, on the other hand, start most games (working groups, partnerships, or projects) without first agreeing on the rules. Everyone has some rules in their own mind, they just don't share them with others. They start the game with the rules tucked away in secret, waiting for someone to break one. When that happens, out comes judgement, blame, and resentment. We assume that any person with half a brain would know about these *common sense, conventional wisdom* rules without us having to spell them out. This is, of course, unfair to our partners. As of this writing, my stepdaughter, Ondine, is eleven years old. She is in the prime "That's not fair" age. I know exactly what to expect if we are playing a game and I introduce a rule without first clearing the rule with her. Let me tell you, I have been *it* a lot.

I was working with one company to improve teamwork when one team member, Lynette, approached me. She said that everything would be fine on her team if it wasn't for Judy. When I asked why, Lynette said, "Judy never gets her time sheets to me by three o'clock every Thursday." I asked, "Did you tell Judy you wanted them by three o'clock each Thursday?" Lynette said, "No, but she should know!" I asked,

"Does she know that you are upset by this?" Lynette said, "I haven't said anything, but come on, it should be obvious." Finally I said, "Judy seems like a nice person. I'll bet if you two agreed on the rules about how to handle the time sheets from now on, everything would be fine. Why don't we go talk to her right now?" Lynette's face flushed, "Oh I couldn't just come right out and tell her that." With that, Lynette beat feet to the other side of the room. I don't know if the time sheet issue ever got solved, but it was apparent that Lynette was comfortable holding everyone else accountable for the rules she created, but not comfortable enough to tell people what those rules were.

Companies would do themselves a favor by not assuming everyone understands the rules the same way. I was conducting a workshop on professional networking skills that had five generations of working adults in one room. The event was sponsored by two different professional associations, but was being held on a university campus, and was also open to a high school business class. In one room there were Traditionalists (a.k.a. "The Silent Generation," born 1925-1942), Baby Boomers (born 1943-1964), Generation X (born 1965-1985), Generation Y (a.k.a. "Millenials," born 1986-2000), and Generation Z (born 2001-present).

As we discussed networking etiquette, what was perceived as common knowledge for some generations was greeted with eye-rolls by another. Half-way through the workshop a high school girl stopped me and admitted, "I have never actually been taught how to give a handshake." It was a good reminder to the older professionals that something they were taught early in life by either their parents or a business mentor might not be as commonplace anymore. We talked about how important a handshake is in making a good impression (not too limp, but not bone-crushing), how to read the other person's signals (how long a hand shake lasts before it becomes creepy), cultural differences (allowing greater personal space for some countries, and closer distances for others), and eye contact (in some countries direct eye contact is necessary, while others consider it rude).

With all the complexities involved in a simple handshake, leaving interactions between staff and customers to chance is not a risk worth taking. Dozens of managers have told me over the years that they just want to find employees who possess "common sense," but given the varying interpretations of what constitutes "sense," expecting us to share a common perception of it is unreasonable. A Human Resources Director at a large theme park told me, "We hire a lot of younger employees. For many of them this is their first job. Because parents don't seem to be talking to their kids these days about what it means to get and keep a job, a lot of our efforts during their first few months of employment is actually spent teaching them how to be an employee. After that we can move on to teaching them how to do their job."

The pressure to hire just the right person puts a lot of stress on Human Resource professionals. (I don't like the term *Human*

Resources. People are not a human version of a resource. That's why I like Southwest Airlines; they replaced the title of Director of Human Resources with President of People.) In all fairness to HR professionals, it is next to impossible to determine, in the span of a few interviews, whether someone is a good fit for the company emotionally and culturally. That is why I think interviews are inadequate. They should be accompanied with an *audition*. Consider this unlikely hiring scenario for a theatre company:

Joseph, a director at a respected theatre is casting actors for the Shakespeare classic, *King Lear* and he is desperate to find just the right actor to play the part of Lear, King of Britain. Since this is the pivotal role of the play, Joseph needs to make sure the actor could not only handle the weight of the role, but will respond well if any unexpected problems pop up during the performance. About two dozen actors apply who are eager for the role. Joseph sets up two chairs in the center of the stage and calls in the first candidate, Nathan. Nathan takes a seat and hands Joseph his resume. After reading over Nathan's performance history Joseph says, "Well, it looks as if you have a lot of experience with Shakespeare, but how familiar are you specifically with the role of Lear?" Nathan thinks for a moment and says, "I haven't actually performed this role, but I think my experience in similar roles would make me a good fit." Joseph asks, "What work have you done that is similar to Lear?" Nathan says, "I played Duncan, the King of Scotland in *Macbeth*, and Caesar in *Julius Caesar*."

Knowing that teamwork is crucial in the theatre, Joseph asks, "If you were to have a problem with one of your fellow actors, how would you handle the situation?" Nathan says, "Before involving any outside parties I like to speak to the other actor first. If we weren't able to resolve the issue, I would ask for a meeting with the two of us and the stage manager. (The Stage Manager is a position of leadership in the theatre world.) If that didn't work, then I would speak to you about it." Joseph says, "That sounds good. Now let's deal with a hypothetical situation. Say you were in the middle of the second act of the play in front of a sold-out house. One of the actors has forgotten his line, a line that is crucial in cueing you for your line, what would you do?"

The conversation goes on for a while and Joseph, satisfied with all of Nathan's responses, says, "It appears that you have everything we need for this role. I will speak with some of your former directors, and if they don't have anything negative to say, the role is yours." Nathan is surprised. He asks, "Don't you want me to audition?" "That's not necessary," says Joseph. "I think I know all I need to know about you."

If you think this would be foolish way to cast a major character in a play, replace the scenario with a typical job interview and you have how almost every employee in America is hired. I believe that, unless you are psychic, interviews are an insufficient way to learn about people. Interviews are really just opportunities for the prospect to tell you what you want to hear. It is pretty rare that a candidate is foolish enough to say things that would expose himself as lazy, uncooperative, or ill-suited for the job. And asking someone what they *would* do in a situation is a far cry from what they would *actually* do.

Auditions are a common practice in theatre, music, and dance because it would be ludicrous to take someone's word about their own abilities in those fields. Everyone wants the job, so of course everyone will say they are perfect for the part. If this is true for the arts, it is true everywhere. I believe that interviews should work side by side with auditions. Once you have reviewed the candidate's resume, you need to be assured that he or she has the right personality for the job. In Jim Collins's words, you need to make sure this is the right person to let on the bus. You need to test real-world skills, which can only be accomplished by a real-world test. Scenarios should be created to test the abilities of the candidate. I have worked with many industries and found very few cases where an audition of sorts wasn't helpful. Even if you are hiring an electrician to be part of a construction crew, you need to go beyond the candidate's knowledge of wiring and electrical code. All employees, no matter what their job, need to work well with a team. An audition for the electrician could involve putting him on a job site where he participates on a project. Other members of the crew would be instructed to interact with the candidate, perhaps even throw some gentle curve balls at him—a last-minute change in the blueprint, an uncooperative co-worker, the client shows up on the job site and isn't happy with the work. Seeing how the candidate reacts in these situations would tell the manager a lot about whether he is a good fit for the crew. This may seem, of course, like a lot of work on your part and a lot of hoops to jump through for the candidate. It also sounds a bit goofy. After all, no one else does it this way. You're right; almost no one adds an audition to the interview process. They replace the risk of extra work and an unusual hiring process with the risk of allowing a bad employee into their company; destroying team morale, lowering productivity, wasting managers' time trying to make the bad fit into a good one, losing customers or clients, alienating co-workers, hurting the company's image, and ultimately firing the employee anyway. Consider the impact that wrong employee can have when they are placed in positions that carry legal implications and you might re-consider whether more time spent during the hiring process is worth it.

At the Mall of America, we helped the hiring managers create real-world scenarios to hire security officers. Candidates had to audition by reacting to scenarios played out by mall employees; a frenzied mother who had lost her child, an unruly guest, and so on. This is similar to the practice runs that emergency professionals conduct, where actors and volunteers portray victims of accidents or disasters so EMTs and first responders can test their skills in a real-life atmosphere.

Sure, candidates can put on their best face for an audition as well as for an interview, but an audition that is realistic is a lot harder to fake. All jobs require unique skills and personality traits, an audition lets those come out. When working with the MOA security force I played the part of an uncooperative mall guest or a frantic father of a missing child. I made sure to test the skills of the officer by not going along with his or her prepared script. Anytime I felt like he was trying to control me during the situation I resisted his direction. In some cases, the candidate who looked really good during the interview didn't fare so well with uncooperative people.

I certainly didn't become a columnist for the Business Journal Newspapers through an interview. Back in 1997 I sent the editor four sample columns for consideration. Luckily, I passed the audition, but the editor didn't just assume I knew the rules of the game. The rules were simple; first, keep my columns under 1500 words. If I didn't, he would shorten the column for me. If I didn't want someone else changing my message, I had to follow the 1500-word rule. Second, be truthful. Finally, be respectful. If I had a criticism to make of a business, don't mention the company by name. If I offered praise for a company I could use the company name, but criticisms should be meant as a heads-up to the readers about mistakes they should avoid, not about what one business did wrong. Calling a company on the carpet by name is just using the media to get revenge. My understanding of the rules—both the simple nuts and bolts as well the deeper implications—has helped me keep a good partnership with the Business Journals.

Getting the right people on the bus, as Jim Collins points out, is the key to a successful business. Don't leave this important task to a simple review of a resume.

Train:
Whose Job Is This Anyway?

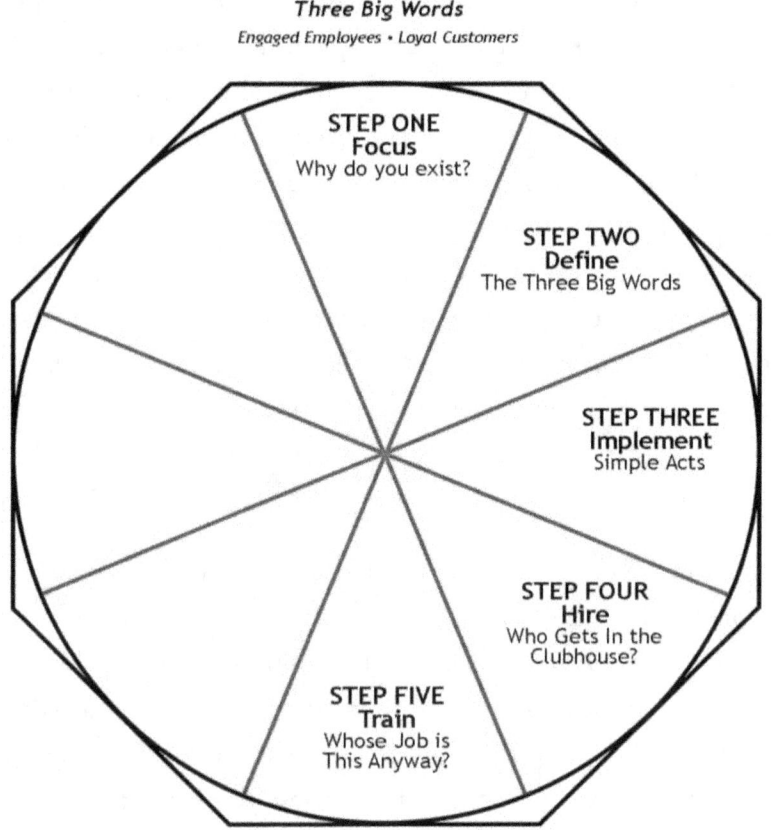

Training new employees to accept an initiative is a lot easier that getting existing employees to move in a new direction. And the odd thing about human nature is, getting people to move in a positive direction always seems more difficult than getting people to act negatively. In order to get thousands of people in India to engage in peaceful protest rather than violent outbursts, Mahatma Ghandi spent a lifetime travelling the country delivering speeches and holding rallies. In some cases, in order to halt violent acts, he engaged in hunger strikes. Dr. Martin Luther King did the same to keep the civil rights movement in America on the path of peace. However, all it takes to incite a riot is to have a favorite team lose a soccer match. On a personal level, it takes constant encouragement to maintain a lifestyle of healthy eating and exercise. All it takes is one ice cream commercial on TV to set those goals aside for "just one cone."

The same wiring in our brains that affects the decision between violence and peace affects our workplace behavior. This neural wiring is the product of eons of evolution, so if you think that showing employees a video or taking them through a half-day orientation session is enough to put them on the right track and keep them there, think again. Group thinking—and its evil cousin, mob mentality—will always be a more powerful force than any authority figure, unless that authority figure understands how the brain is wired and can use that wiring to good advantage. In the book, *Social: Why Our Brains Are Wired to*

Connect, Matthew Lieberman explains why. Lieberman is a Harvard University graduate and professor in the Departments of Psychology, Psychiatry, and Bio-behavioral Sciences at the University of California in Los Angeles. He is also the founding editor of the journal *Social Cognitive and Affective Neuroscience*. He is a pioneer in a comparatively new field of study, social neuroscience. Lieberman states that, although people believe that humans became the dominant species on the planet by virtue of speech, the written word, opposable thumbs, and country line dancing, our real advantage came from the fact that our brains are wired to create social networks with those around us. In fact, even though all mammals live and work in social groups, the human brain is wired interact on a much more complex social level than any other mammal on the plant.

Being small and weak in the animal world was indeed mitigated by our ability to fashion tools and weapons, but even with a good spear, a single human is no match for a mastodon (or a ten-year-old at an *American Girl* store). So our brains evolved with the ability to detect subtle signals from others and to change our behavior in order to create advantages for the group. This results in humans having a keen awareness of our place in social and working groups. In short, we are more concerned about how others view our behavior than we are about our own opinion. We like to think that, as individuals, we weigh the pros and cons of various options and decide what is best for us. In fact, more often than not we simply go with the group. Those who don't are considered to have an anti-social disorder. These people become snow-plow drivers who come by just after you have shoveled your driveway.

An interesting experiment detailed in Lieberman's book was conducted to test the boundaries of our tendency to go with the group. Snacks were placed in workplace break rooms with no attendant present to collect money for the treats. An "honor system" box was placed next to the treats with the prices listed for each treat. The amount of treats lost to theft were tracked over a period of time. Then, the same treats were placed in the same break rooms, but with a mirror placed so that the employees could see themselves when they bought (or stole) a treat. The number of thefts dropped dramatically. Apparently it is not much fun to cheat when you can see yourself committing the crime. Then the researchers took the test a step further. They replaced the mirror with a poster of a person's face looking at you. Even though it was the face of an unknown person, instead of your own face looking back at you in a mirror, thefts remained low. Not only don't we like watching ourselves commit a crime, we don't like the perception of others watching us. To take the test a step further the poster of the human face was replaced with one that just had two eyes looking at you; thefts still remained low. One step further, the same result occurred when the poster was replaced with one that only had three dots in a triangle; two on top simulating eyes, and one on the bottom simulating a mouth. As long is the appearance of a face was present, crime was inhibited. When the poster was rotated so the single dot was on top—when the appearance of eyes and a mouth disappeared—so did the treats.

The number of thefts returned to the same as when there was no poster at all.

What does all this talk about mirrors, dots, faces, and group mentality have to do with training employees? It means that you can't expect to accomplish anything by training the individual employee; you must create a group mentality. Companies typically have a group training day, where everyone sits and learns about general company policy. Then a manager will take the individual and conduct training for the specific job. Or a new hire will shadow a more experienced employee. These are not necessarily bad choices, but they are not sufficient in creating the kind of attitude you need in the new employee. In one company where I was conducting workshops, the manager said, "We always get new employees who are bright-eyed and eager. They go through the orientation and are excited to hit the floor and take on their new jobs. But all it takes is a few shifts of working next to a fellow employee who is sour and angry and the *new employee shine* wears right off. It is almost like the older employees hate to see someone else happy."

I had a personal experience with this when I was younger. To earn money for college I worked for a summer with the street maintenance department in my hometown of Rochester, Minnesota. (Tip to parents: if you want to make sure your child goes to college, have him spend time filling potholes and driving dump trucks.) As you might expect, I was the young kid surrounded by men who would spend their entire adult life working for the city (women weren't hired for this kind of work when I was a kid). I was raised by parents who valued a hard day's work so I was eager to carry my weight. My workmates, however, knew that no matter how many streets they re-paved, pot holes they filled, or curbs they fixed, there would always be more waiting the next day. So they were a bit less eager about the job than I.

We were scheduled to have a twenty-minute break in the morning and afternoon, and a forty-five minute break for lunch. On my first day, at the twenty minute mark of the morning break, I jumped to my feet and said, "Okay. What's next?" The other guys gave me a look like I had just suggested we all go to the opera. The foreman, the oldest and crankiest guy on the crew, said, "I don't know where you're going, but we'll tell you when it's time to work." For the rest of the summer, I don't remember a break that lasted less than half an hour or a lunch that didn't stretch to well over an hour. The chief of all the crews spent his time driving from site to site telling foremen to get their crews to get back to work. I think my first taste of real irony was when one of my crew mates said, "All that guy does is go around telling people to work. The city could save a lot of money if they fired him." This was said just before the crewman dozed off to sleep in the cab of his truck. It thought back to those days as I spoke with the woman who said that her new employees' eagerness was soured by the bad attitudes of older employees. I know that, if I had stayed on that street maintenance crew, I would be sleeping in the cab of a dump truck right now. There is no way my parent's hard work in raising a conscientious, hard-working young man could have stood against the pressure of a group of co-workers I would face every day. To expect different of any employee is unreasonable, and unrealistic.

An important concept discussed in the book, *Influencer*, is that of the "Opinion Leader." Authors Grenney et al. discovered that any initiative in which the leaders of an organization tried to use authority as the sole tool for positive change was doomed to failure. Opinion leaders are those in the organization who may not have title or official authority, but they hold sway over the opinions of their colleagues. The opinion leader phenomenon starts as soon as we are born. Remember when you were in school and the teacher was talking to the class? As soon as class let out you ran over to your best friend and asked, "What do *you* think about what the teacher said?" The same thing happens at work every day. As soon as the boss leaves the room, employees look to the person whose opinion they value and ask for guidance.

If you don't know who the opinion leaders are in your organization, just keep your eyes open. They will be the ones the staff circles around at meetings, on break, or at events. They are not necessarily the most vocal, and they don't always point themselves out, but they are easy to spot if you really look. If you want the Three Big Words to be effective, get the opinion leaders on board first.

Next, be sure of the ultimate outcome you are looking for, not just the tasks of the job. There is a big difference between explaining the job and really training the employee. At Disney-owned theme parks around the world, an apprentice-based program is part of all training, no matter what the position is. Disney takes a purposeful approach in using opinion leaders; in effect, they encourage the positive side of Lieberman's social neurology. Whereas some companies choose mentors or trainers based on seniority, Disney selects mentors to train apprentice employees based on attitude. They know that whatever attitude the mentor has about the job will show up quickly in the new hire. And once in place, attitude is hard to change; so you better start with the right one.

Disney apprenticeships go beyond the simple tasks of the job. In a video training session I attended as an observer, an older employee at Walt Disney World in Florida was showing an apprentice the ropes of his new job, clean-up crew. The two were dressed in sharp white uniforms with black bow ties. They roamed the park with small brooms and dustpans sweeping up trash. When the video first started I thought, "Do you really need an apprentice-ship to learn how to sweep up trash? Just hand him a broom and say, 'Here. Go find trash.'" What I saw next made all the difference. While the older man and younger apprentice walked and swept, the older one said, "Now right around here is where people always seem to lose purses and bags. So you want to know that the lost and found is past that building over there so you can give our guests good directions. And the restrooms are right over there. Since we're by some restaurants, people ask about that when you are in this area." The entire time, the older mentor never talked about the trash they were sweeping up. Instead, he talked about the nature of their work; their roles as ambassadors for the park; how they did much more than keep the place clean, they helped people enjoy what could likely be the biggest trip of their lives.

I have told clients, "I can train a monkey to do almost any job, but I can't train a monkey to serve people and solve problems." People respond to reward and punishment, and the risk of losing something is more powerful than the chance of winning. In his book, *Influence: Science and Practice*, Dr. Robert Cialdini discovered this fact in real terms. When residents of California were approached by volunteers to participate in energy saving activities, some were told they could *save* fifty cents a day if they engaged in the new practices; others were told they would *lose* fifty cents a day if they didn't. The group that was worried about losing money far outpaced the group that was promised a gain. Beyond reward and punishment, however, people are most concerned about fitting in with the group. In a similar study about energy savings, some residents were told to save energy because it was the right thing to do for the planet and future generations. Others were told that it would save the resident money. And a third group was told, in so many words, that "everyone else is doing it." When asked which reason would most likely be the one to affect their decision to engage in energy saving practices, people believed their reason would be to save the planet (saving energy was the right thing to do). The next most common reason was that it would save money. Almost no one believed they would act based on what other people were doing. The unique part of the test was that each neighborhood was separated by utility billing, so the researchers could send specific promotional to each neighborhood and follow up to see who was following the energy saving practices. The residents who engaged in the most energy saving behaviors were the ones who received the promotional materials specifically related to "other people are doing it." Even those who thought they would not act based on others' behavior were most influenced by social pressure. No matter what the incentive, we will do what those around us do. Managers and training directors would do well to keep this in mind. Training individuals is fine for imparting particular skills, but attitude and decision making is a group thing.

Training for the true nature of the job and not the tasks of the job should focus on the true nature of the entire organization. This helps people see themselves as part of something bigger than themselves. I saw this in practice at a workshop I conducted at a large casino. I was walking through the lobby on my way to the auditorium to conduct a session for a company that was meeting at the casino. I had on a business suit and was carrying my attaché case (yes, I still use one). My eyes were directed straight ahead and my pace was quick; it was obvious I wasn't there to play. Suddenly I heard a voice from behind me, "Hey! Are you here to have some fun?" I turned to see who it was, expecting to see a hotel desk clerk or concierge. I was shocked. It was a security guard. A twenty-something, male, fully armed, uniformed with a hat, security guard. He repeated, "Are you here to play?" "No," I said. "I'm doing a workshop in your auditorium." He smiled and said, "That's great, but remember we are here for people to have fun. So when you finish with your work, don't leave without treating yourself to a game or two."

We have all been in the presence of a typical security guard. Many of them take the job because they like the trappings of the position; the uniform, the authority, the firearms. They don't usually smile at you when you walk by. They follow you with a cold stare that says, "I've got my eye on you." Here was a young man who was willing to set all that aside and focus on the real nature of the organization—fun—and he made sure people coming to a place of fun actually had fun. No one says, "Honey, I want to go to *Big Casino* because I feel so secure there." What was the impact of that one security guard? That encounter took place in 2002 and I remember it like it was yesterday. Had I the spare time I would have tracked down the director of security and asked him or her how they produced such a perfect example of what employees should be like. I wanted to ask all about their training. I wanted to know how they rewarded such behavior. I didn't have the time; after all, I wasn't there to have fun you know.

I saw the same thing happen at the Mall of America after we got the employees thinking about the real reason the mall existed. A member of the maintenance crew was driving his golf-cart maintenance vehicle on the way to a repair job when he saw a woman being trailed by a gaggle of kids. Sometimes parents offer to take their friends' kids to the mall and act as chaperone. This gives the other parents a free day and earns the chaperone a place in the Parents Hall of Fame. This woman, however, was also weighed down by a ton of shopping bags. Apparently just riding the rollercoaster wasn't enough for the kids, they wanted to go shopping! She looked like she was just about to collapse. The maintenance crewman saw this and stopped. "Hi there," he said. "Are you on your way out?" With the kids running around her the woman said, "Thank God, yes." The crewman said, "Safety rules won't allow us to have anyone ride on the cart with me, but I'll tell you what. You put all those bags on my cart and I'll follow you out to your car in the parking ramp." If the woman wasn't already married, the crewman probably would have received a marriage proposal on the spot. How many people do you think that woman told about her experience? How many saw a Facebook post or Twitter feed about it?

This is about more than simply training employees to look for meaningful moments to do more than their tasks, it is about giving them the power to do so. When Gordon Bethune took the reins at Continental Airlines in 1994 the company was in deep trouble. Continental had already been to bankruptcy court twice and was on its way for a third time. Three times to bat for a company that size usually means the end. In 1994, Continental was noted as having the worst record in the airline industry for the three metrics that mattered most; on time arrivals, lost luggage, and passenger satisfaction. Bethune did a number of strategic changes in the company, and within one year Continental had bounced back and had achieved the highest ratings in the industry; quite a feat for an organization employing thousands of people.

One thing that Bethune did that stymied his colleagues was to free his employees from the rule book. His first act a President and CEO was to take the entire library of employee manuals, dump them in a 55-gallon metal drum in the parking lot of the company's headquarters, and light them on fire. He said, "An employee can't go to the bathroom at Continental without having to check the employee handbook." His philosophy was simple; hire good people and trust them to do their best work. He set high expectations, but rather than whip people into shape, he rewarded them into shape. He created a culture that attracted the kind of people who wanted to serve the passenger, the same way Herb Kelleher attracted the right kind of employee to Southwest Airlines in 1967.

Another of Bethune's policies that drew skepticism was empowering any employee—gate clerks, flight attendants, pilots, anyone—to do whatever it took to make a disgruntled passenger happy. Colleagues told Bethune he was crazy. They said that employees would give away airline miles like there was no tomorrow. Bethune stood by his belief that employees are generally reasonable and responsible. He asked his employees to, when pleasing an unhappy passenger, please start small. Offer a coupon for a free dessert in the airport food court, or some kind of special treatment while on board. He reminded them that if they gave away the farm, soon there would be no farm to work for. Only in extreme cases should free airline tickets be used as a gift. It worked. Continental employees honored Bethune's trust in them by starting with small gifts to please an unhappy passenger. It turned out that a free ice-cream cone from the food court was all most people needed to feel better. Who can blame them? After all, we're talking about ice cream!

The Mall of America did something similar by giving the housekeeping staff "goodie bags" to attach to the cleaning cart. If a housekeeping employee encountered a troubled guest, the employee was free to dig into a goodie-bag and offer a food coupon, ride tickets, or other treat. What costs the mall a few pennies creates good will that is worth a fortune. And employees reported that they actually felt less stressed about their job because they had something tangible to offer a troubled guest; certainly something more tangible than, "Sorry you're having a bad day. I got to go clean now." Along these lines, studies have shown that people enjoy surprises even more if the gift is not attached to a mistake. Although it is nice to offer something in return for a poor experience, it is often expected. Since it is common to offer something to compensate for a mistake, the gift can lose impact. If, however, a restaurant manager surprises a guest by saying, "I've seen you in here a lot. For being so loyal, dessert is on me tonight," the gift means more because she is not trying to make up for a mistake.

Stevie Ray's Improv Company offers a surprise to the guests who attend a corporate workshop. Even though we are paid a fee by the client to conduct our training sessions, and the employees are most often paid to be there (since they are on the clock), we will sometimes give the attendees free tickets to Stevie Ray's Comedy Cabaret. This comes as a complete surprise to the client, and it is the kind of surprise people love to receive.

Keep this in mind when training employees. Tell them to be on the look-out for fun opportunities to surprise customers, not just react to bad situations.

Good training is not a one-time, now-you-know-your-job-so-go-do-it approach. Training cannot be focused only on those who are climbing the company ladder, which is often the case. Your front line employees need ongoing support to help the company remain successful. And the training cannot be solely focused on how well they perform their tasks, it must include the One Reason You Exist. Training is all about communication. However, all too often, once the initial training is completed the only communication is on how to do the job, not why the job is important. If you recall the research conducted on *distributed teams*, it was discovered that the best way to maintain morale and productivity among working groups that were geographically dispersed was communication that was both frequent and spontaneous. The same is necessary for all teams; distributed or otherwise. Contact with leadership that is unplanned and frequent helps staff members avoid slipping into the mundane of day-to-day tasks.

Remember the story of Emma, the little girl who just wanted to ride the rides at the Mall of America? MOA employees may not know it, but there is an Emma at the mall every day. There is also a tired woman trying to keep track of an energetic bunch of kids while carrying arm-loads of shopping bags. The most important lesson employees must learn during training is to know that they will encounter an Emma every day. They will encounter a stressed parent every day. They will encounter someone for whom this is the first time that customer has ever experienced what you are providing. The first plane ride, the first time buying a house, the first oil change, the first tax return, or maybe even the first time eating in a restaurant. Your employees only have one chance to make that first time perfect.

I was asked to conduct a workshop on communication skills for a group of parents. The unique thing about these parents was that they all had children with special needs, some parents had more than one special needs child in the home. My session was part of a weekend long conference designed to help them better cope with the stresses of raising special needs kids. I call these wonderful people *Special Parents*. The conference was held at a hotel. While talking with some of the Special Parents after my session, I learned that for many of them this was the first time they had been out of their house since their child was born. The overwhelming costs of caring for special needs children meant that the parents went to work, came home, and cared for their child. That was it; day after day, year after year. What was for me a typical hotel stay was, for these Special Parents, the weekend of a lifetime. After than conversation, I try to keep those parents, and Emma, in mind every time I speak to a group.

We train members of Stevie Ray's Improv Company to look for the Emma's we might encounter in our work. The troupe members who perform at Stevie Ray's Comedy Cabaret could easily see the shows as being just a night of entertainment for our guests. However, we remind them that there are people in the audience for whom this might be the only night in years that they get to do something just for themselves. It is easy for employees to recognize big events in customers' lives. A flight attendant might announce that a couple on the plane is celebrating their 50th wedding anniversary. Or a cupcake with a candle might be delivered to a restaurant guest accompanied by "Happy Birthday" sung by the servers. But the real Emma's don't always announce themselves.

To find out if there are Emmas in our audience, we ask. Our website states, "If you are celebrating anything special, let us know and we will do something in the show just for you." When guests make reservations by phone, the box office staff is encouraged to ask if there is any special reason for attending the show. The information is included in a show report that is given to the troupe each night. It lists the name and table number of the guest as well as information about their reason for attending. When we started this practice, we expected to hear about birthdays and anniversaries. What surprised us were the other celebrations that were just as important; "Our child has just returned from college for the summer," "My wife is cancer-free for the first time in ten years," and "Our son is home from being deployed overseas for fifteen months." One night, a table full of women were having a rowdy good time and the troupe assumed it was just another ladies night out. After the show, one of the women approached them and said, "We are all sisters here with our mother. Our father died almost a year ago and mom hasn't been out since then. We finally got her to spend an evening with her daughters. You made her laugh for the first time since dad died; and we can't thank you enough." Emmas are everywhere.

Earlier I told the story of Curt, the agoraphobic who took improv classes to gain the confidence to conquer his fear of the outdoors. Over the years, we have discovered other Curts and Emmas in the School of Improv. One of our instructors, Emily, had just finished teaching an eight-week Beginning Improv course to sixteen students. Our students range in age from late teens to the early '90s, and this group was similarly a mixed bunch. They all gathered in the lounge after the class to celebrate. Emily is a lover of improvisation, so she is always interested in what drives folks to the art. While the group relaxed and chatted, Emily asked what prompted each student to try improv. I mentioned earlier that we ask new students the reason for them deciding to join, but you can get markedly different answers after developing a relationship over a few months. After a few people responded with the usual "To try something new," and "To improve my quick-thinking skills for work" Drew spoke up. Drew was a guy in his mid-forties and had never done anything like this before. He said, "A few months ago I walked in on my wife in bed with another guy." The class gasped, but he added, "...for the third time." Now the students were in shock. He continued, "The third time was the charm and we decided to get divorced. My whole life was pulled apart. I didn't know what to do and I had no one to talk to, so I decided to take this class to get out of the house. I can honestly say that, if I didn't have these classes to look forward to every Tuesday night, I don't know how I would have made it through all that." Not only are Emma's everywhere, they come with many different stories.

One of the core principles of improvisation is to support every idea and suggestion created by your fellow student or troupe member. The rule is, you must accept what is given and add to their idea by including your own. It is a concept known in improv as, *"Yes, and."* The rule of "Yes, and" tries to replace the tendency to "Yeah, but…" an idea you don't like. "Yeah, but" is one of the most common phrases in the English language. Our brain is wired to instantly compare other people's ideas against what we already know. Since we are more comfortable with the familiar, we commonly reject perfectly good ideas because they are new; strange. So we say, "I see your point, but…" or "I can see how you might feel that way, however…" In improvisation these reactions are called a *negation.* To negate someone is to shut down their ideas and force yours. Negations include "but," "however," and the big daddy of them all, "No!"

One of the most difficult skills new students of improv learn is to avoid negating their partners and instead accept and incorporate others' ideas into their own. The result is an atmosphere that is much more cooperative. This results in a group that is also more productive and creative. A common comment we hear from students is that they have never been in an environment in which their ideas were accepted so readily without criticism or judgement. You can imagine how this kind of *yes* environment affected Drew, who had likely endured years of living in a marriage filled with *no* (and one big yes that was a lie, "I do."). After Drew shared his story, other students opened up about how the class helped them through difficult life situations. Emily had no idea what impact a simple improv class had on the lives of her students.

The thing about the Emmas of the world—the Special Parents, the student facing a painful divorce, or the family celebrating the life of a lossed loved one—is that you rarely know who they are. Does your training go beyond tasks and duties? Does it reflect the true depth and scope of the work and what it means to those the organization serves? Do you train your employees to look for Emma?

Coach:
Lead by Example

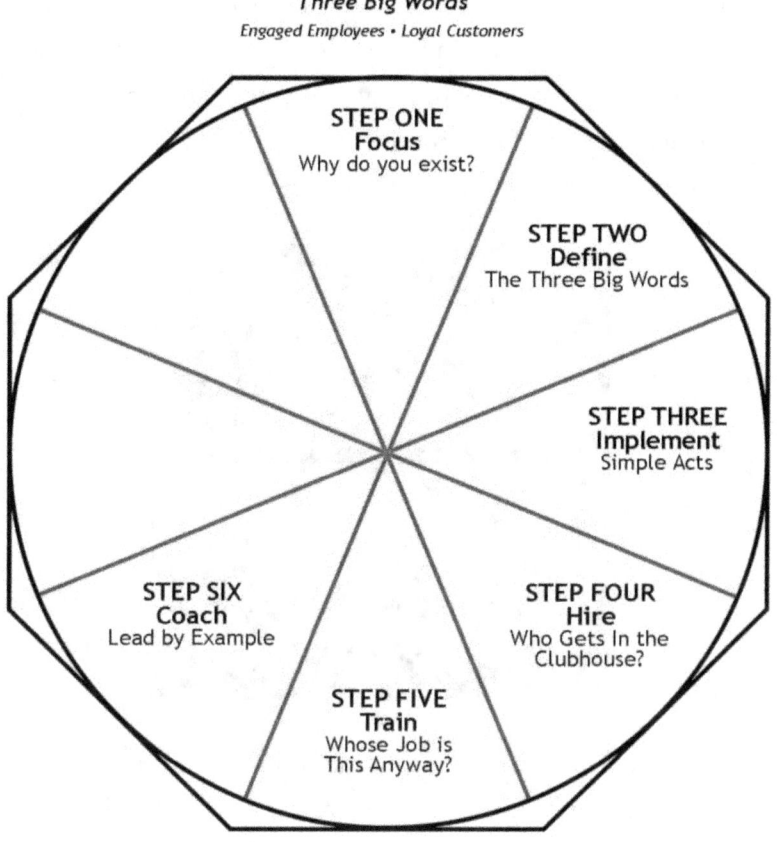

There is no shortage of books on leadership. These books fall into two general categories. The first involves a successful CEO who decides that he or she has become so successful that he or she should write a book entitled "This is how I did it. You should do the same." The problem is that little research goes into the book. The author uses personal/professional experience and anecdotes to prove his point, and has the luxury of ignoring any evidence to the contrary of "This is how things ought to be done."

The other type of leadership book is written by a consultancy firm or think-tank. These can be well researched, but may lack real world application, depending on whether the pages and pages of footnotes are backed up by someone in the organization having been in a leadership position outside of the lab.

The qualities that make an effective leader are influenced by many factors; the culture of the organization, the self-awareness of the individual, and the atmosphere in which the individual was raised. Regardless of the factors that created the individual, the style of leadership that is most appropriate is based entirely on the type of team being led and current circumstances the organization is facing. Adjusting to the needs of the group can only occur with leaders who are both self-aware and who have the experience necessary to adjust their approach to meet the needs of the team. This skill is rare.

The problem with most leadership advice is that people believe that only one type of leadership is the right kind. This has created a culture in which the *style de jour* is touted, and whatever came before is vilified. For example, for generations good leadership was thought to emulate the military. Military command-and-control style of leadership is perfect for certain environments and situations, but it isn't the be-all, end-all of leadership. The next wave, the servant leader, came about in an attempt to create a more humane and caring workplace. This is a wonderful goal, until the servant leader is not what is called for. Below I will discuss the most common styles of leadership. You will see which best describes you, but even more importantly, you should examine your ability to adapt to the style called for by the situation. There is some cross-over of leadership styles in the following pages, but I wanted to offer various perspectives from trusted sources.

Going Against the Tide

Before getting into the various styles of leadership, we should recognize that it takes courage to decide for one's self which approach is appropriate. If you choose what you feel is right, count on someone disagreeing with you. An example of one leader who did not let outside forces or a traditional model of leadership influence him was Henry Ford. Ford stood apart from other business leaders of his day, as well as the prevailing attitude of employer-employee relations. Ford was born in 1863, making him a young adult when John D. Rockefeller was creating his Standard Oil monopoly in the early 1880s. Rockefeller was a traditional 19th century leader in that he was authoritarian and autocratic. He was widely known for being tough on employees, employing union busters, and using violent methods to control his workforce. Given Rockefeller's fame, Ford would have certainly been aware of Rockefeller's business practices and philosophy. However, when Ford was building his automobile company his leadership style was wholly different than Rockefeller's. First, Ford believed in the power of a happy workforce. He paid his workers higher than the average salary of the time and instituted the eight-hour work day. He once said, "There is one rule for the industrialist and that is: make the best quality goods possible at the lowest cost possible, paying the highest wages possible."

Ford also pioneered diversity in the workplace, at one point employing over 62 different nationalities, over 900 people with disabilities, and he was one of the few to start employing women. Ford demonstrated a high degree of emotional intelligence. His motivation for selling cars at low cost was not simply to increase the number of potential customers. He believed that people would feel better emotionally if they could afford something as life-changing as independent transportation. His philosophy was, "If there is any one secret of success, it lies in the ability to get the other person's point of view and see things from that person's angle, as well as your own." Rockefeller built a successful company relying upon the traditional leader style of his day. Ford found success by transforming how leadership was viewed from that day forward.

If you do indeed want to buck tradition, you are attempting to innovate. Depending on the organization you work for, this may run counter to other leaders who were raised with the command and control style of leadership (where the boss says "Jump" and the employees ask "How high?"). Paul Sloane, head of the British Quality Foundation's Innovation Unit and author of *The Innovative Leader: How to Inspire Your Team and Drive Creativity*, identifies an inspirational leader as being more innovative. He believes that a command and control leader will use checks and controls, whereas an innovative leader will trust and delegate. A command and control leader will value operational over strategic issues; the innovative leader is the opposite. A command and control leader treats employees as subordinates; an innovative leader treats staff as colleagues. A command and control leader can be very decisive, but will often make decisions without soliciting input, whereas an innovative leader will seek advice from colleagues and staff. The goal of the team, in the eyes of a command and control leader, is to execute policy and implement plans. The innovative leader, on the other hand, sees the purpose of a team as being creative.

Other key differences between command and control and innovative leaders, according to Sloan, is how they hire and reward staff. A command and control leader will hire based on experience, qualifications, and track-record. An innovative leader will hire staff based on attitude, creativity, and capabilities. Command and control leaders reward based solely on performance, whereas innovative leaders reward entrepreneurial actions. As a whole, command and control leaders avoid risk, discourage dissent, and are more numbers-oriented and analytical. Innovative leaders are prone to take more calculated risks, encourage constructive criticism from staff, and are more intuitive and ideas-oriented. Finally, a command and control leader dislikes any sign of failure. An innovative leader, while not unconcerned with failure, is more comfortable with it being part of the growth process. Sloane points out that a command and control style of leadership does have its benefits. For instance, it is well-suited for improving operational efficiency in a well-defined environment, which is certainly the case for some organizations.

Leadership is at the core of the book, *First Break All the Rules*, by Marcus Buckingham and Curt Coffman. The book was the result of a ten-year project by the Gallup Organization to answer one question, "What makes companies profitable?" Using a process called meta-analysis, Buckingham and Coffman were able to whittle away every factor of a business's operation that, while important, did not ultimately affect profitability. After a decade of research, they discovered that the one factor of a business that had the most impact on profitability was employee happiness. Not employee *satisfaction*, employee *happiness*.

Buckingham and Coffman recognized that leaders must rely on certain steps in order to create a functional workplace, but the very title of the book is based on the fact that great leaders must never adhere too closely to outdated rules of business (they would have like Henry Ford). "The best managers…know that the manager's challenge is not to perfect people, but to capitalize on each person's uniqueness. They select talent, no matter how simple the role. Their first instinct is to trust the people they have selected." Even though these qualities clearly align with Sloane's description for an innovative leader, Buckingham and Coffman go on to identify other rules for governing an employee's actions. "Employees must follow certain required steps for all aspects of their role that deal with accuracy or safety." "Employees must follow required steps when those steps are part of a company or industry standard."

The outcome of *First Break All the Rules* was a list of twelve questions that any leader or manager could ask to determine if an employee was happy at work. Out of the twelve questions, often referred to as *Q. 12*, only the first two relate to a command and control approach; "Do I know what is expected of me at work?" and "Do I have the materials and equipment I need to do my work right?" The other ten are related to employee success, "At work, do I have the opportunity to do what I do best every day?" or employee engagement, "Does my supervisor, or someone at work, seem to care about me as a person?" or employee growth, "In the last six months, has someone at work talked to me about my progress?" Buckingham and Coffman agree with Sloane that, while the command and control style of leadership is necessary, its scope is narrowly defined; and both styles must support the other.

Another outcome of the Gallup project were follow-up books, *Now Discover Your Strengths*, and *The One Thing You Need to Know*. This trilogy introduced the concept of strengths-based management, where the focus of leadership is on building the employee's strengths rather than wasting time trying to fix weaknesses. Rather than the old style of leadership, which would illuminate weak skills of the employee that "need attention," strengths-based management dictates that any failure on the part of an employee was likely the cause of a manager who put the employee directly in the path of failure. This is not to say that employees cannot falter and, as a result, grow. It simply recognizes that there are no true weaknesses, only areas of business for which an employee is ill-suited. It is a waste of time, energy, and stress to try to force a square peg into a round hole.

Rhea Blanken, with ASAE: The Center for Association Leadership, identifies eight common leadership styles: Charismatic, Innovative, Command and Control, Laissez-Faire, Pace Setter, Servant, Situational, and Transformational. Blanken recognizes that, rather than one style being better than another, they each have a time and place.

A **Charismatic** leader, such as television personality and social leader Oprah Winfrey, influences others based on his or her personality, and motivates others to act. A Charismatic leader may inspire passion in others, but can often believe more in him/herself that in the team. Blanken believes that the best use of a Charismatic leader is when others must be spurred into action, to raise team morale, or to expand an organization's position in the marketplace. The risk, however, is that a team may flounder once the leader is gone. A Charismatic leader may also have such a strong self-image that he or she may take on excessive risk. Also, the team's morale, while boosted in the beginning, may diminish because successes may be attributed to the leader instead of the team.

An **Innovative** leader, such as business tycoon Richard Branson, seeks to bring about new thinking and action by grasping the entirety of a situation and going beyond the usual course of action. This type of leader is good at moving beyond intractable issues and creating a work environment that fosters new ideas. The downside is increased risk of failure for all involved, but this is balanced by the entire team taking satisfaction from successes. Innovative leadership also creates an atmosphere of greater respect for others' ideas.

The **Command and Control** leader, according to Blanken's definition, is characterized by New York Giants head coach, Tom Coughlin. A Command and Control leader follows rules and expects others to do the same. This type of leadership is best used during times of urgency when there is no time for discussion, when safety is at stake, or when needing to meet a strict deadline. The benefit is members clearly understanding their role in the process, however a Command and Control style limits anyone other than the leader from gaining new skills and there is little chance for team members to learn from experiences and improve performance.

The **Laissez-Faire** leader, such as fashion icon Donna Karan, is aware of what is going on in the organization, but does not become directly involved beyond his or her own participation. This leader trusts others to keep to deadlines and promises, but will monitor performance and give regular feedback. This type of leadership is possible when dealing with a highly cohesive team, or for teams that are remotely located. It can also provide quick results. In order for a Laissez-Faire leadership style to be effective the team must be self-directed, especially in time and resources. The autonomy among team members provided by this style of leadership leads to high job satisfaction and increased productivity, but this is only possible with a well-connected team.

The **Pace Setter** leadership style is best exemplified by Jeff Bezos, the founder of Amazon. The Pace Setter leader sets high standards of performance for the group, but seeks to epitomize the same qualities him/herself. In order for a Pace Setter style of leadership to be effective, the team members must be self-motivated and highly skilled. They must also be able to embrace new ideas, new projects, and act quickly. In this type of atmosphere, actions are of the utmost importance, and must lead to results. The Pace Setter style of leadership carries the risk of burning out team members; as such, it can lack sustainability. Sometimes the results needed are outside of the team's ability to match the pace set by the leader.

The **Servant** leader, as demonstrated by Herb Kelleher, co-founder and CEO of Southwest Airlines, puts service to others above his or her own self-interests. Kelleher's philosophy is, "The business of business is people." To discourage the status symbol of his position, he took an interior office with no windows at his headquarters. The Servant leader includes the entire team in decision making and ensures that the team has all the tools they need to reach their goals. Also, the Servant leader does not seek recognition for his or her work, instead allowing the team to accept credit for positive outcomes. This type of leader is appropriate when the leader is elected to the position, rather than assigned. It is also helpful when anyone can meet the needs of the team, regardless of their position. The "Best Places to Work" lists will often have a Servant leader in charge. The result is a staff with a high morale, but this style of leadership is not well suited to situations that need decisive action or quick decisions. The atmosphere under a Servant leader is also challenging when the organization is beset by tight deadlines.

The **Situational** leader can be found in Pat Summit, the women's basketball coach at the University of Tennessee, who holds the record for being the all-time winning coach in NCAA history. The Situational leader balances empowering others with a coaching approach to link the group's readiness with the desired behavior. A Situational leader is best utilized when ongoing procedures need refinement or reinvention. A Situational leader helps reduce uncertainty among the team by demonstrating the ability to adapt to changing circumstances. However, if these changes come too often, and the Situational leader simply changes along with the tide, this can be confusing to the team.

Finally, the **Transformational** leader, as personified by Ben Cohen and Jerry Greenfield, who took a correspondence course in ice cream making and a $12,000 investment and created the internationally known brand, Ben & Jerry's Ice Cream. The Transformational leader expects the team to continually transform, even when it might be uncomfortable. They believe in change for change's sake. A Transformational leader seeks to serve as a role model for the team, and therefore expects a high degree of commitment from the team members. This type of leader, because he or she focuses on innovation and creativity, inspires optimism, enthusiasm, and commitment.

The result is high productivity from team members, but this requires a team that is detail-oriented and able to follow work schedules.

All of the leadership styles listed above have one thing in common, the needs of the team come first; for it is the team members who will ultimately fulfill the goals of the company. For this to work, the employees must be used as a source of insight into the operations of the organization. As a CEO once told me, "I will never ask the janitor his advice about the five-year plan, but if I want to know about how things are going on a day-to-day basis, he is my first choice."

When the Mall of America was in the process of the Three Big Words, I was asked to attend a series of employee meetings to introduce the program. These meetings were held quarterly. One thing that leadership had not done in a while was to reserve some time at the end of each meeting for employee input and suggestions. This may seem like a no-brainer to some, but I have seen hundreds of such meetings where the front-line employees sit silently while the boss reads the new marching orders. Maybe the leaders feel that having a suggestion box in the break room is sufficient opportunity to hear from the rank-and-file. At best, a quick "Any questions or comments?" is tossed out at the end of the meeting. This can usually be translated into "Please don't say anything so we can get out of here."

When the MOA managers opened up the floor, the staff was a bit more willing to engage in conversation because I had just taken them through some hands-on exercises that taught the skills of interaction they would be called upon to use with guests. When employees have to sit silently for an hour and listen, it sends a signal that you don't want their input. However, when a meeting includes group interaction it sends a signal that their participation is welcome. When the floor was opened up for comments a flood of ideas came forth; how to speed up transactions, how to lessen the stress of returning merchandise, and some problems that management didn't even know existed.

The problem with suggestion boxes or online feedback is that people think and react differently when they are alone than when they converse with others. During conversation, one idea sparks another. Conversation spurs memory; issues that are otherwise forgotten by the end of the day are brought to the surface. This very fact is why many managers actually avoid group feedback sessions, they are afraid of the meeting becoming a complaint session. This is certainly a valid concern, but one that is easily handled by agreeing at the outset that "We are here to talk about solutions, not just problems." By the time the MOA quarterly meetings were done, the managers had notepads full of ideas for improvements; all provided free of charge by willing staff members. And, because the ideas came from the employees, they were more eager to help enact the changes.

During the early years of Stevie Ray's Improv Company, Pamela Mayne and I were eager good ideas and business advice, so we attended every workshop we could find. One great session was conducted by a man who owned seven restaurants in the Denver area. To keep even a single restaurant open and profitable is an accomplishment, so we were eager to hear how a guy kept seven successful establishments going without being part of a franchise. We thought he would give us his secrets of managing a business, but most of what he talked about was how to be a good leader.

He asked, "Have you ever noticed that some restaurant managers will walk right by a spill on the floor and not stop to clean it up? They think that lowly task is beneath them, so they tell an employee to 'run over to table fourteen for a clean-up.' The message is loud and clear to the employee that the manager doesn't really care; so why should the employee? So, instead of getting a cheap bar towel to handle the spill, the employee grabs a handful of expensive paper bar napkins and soaks up the mess.

"This is the same manager who will experience higher than average losses due to employee theft, higher than average broken dishes from servers' sloppy handling, and flatware tossed in the trash because of inattentive bus workers. Leaders get from their staff exactly what they demonstrate in their own behavior." I thought about his workshop the day that the Mall of America directors went on the *Mall Walk* with me. The goal was to practice engaging with the guests, not to patrol the mall, but I still saw the directors themselves bending over to pick up any little bit of trash they saw on the floor. They eagerly engaged in the kind of behavior they wanted their employees to practice. They sent a message to the entire staff that no one is above serving the good of the organization.

The difference between a leader and a manager is that the manager enforces policy while the leader creates a vision. A vision is something great that does not yet exist. John F. Kennedy stated one vision he had for his presidency, "Put a man on the moon by 1970." Moon missions were not yet possible, so this was a vision of something that did not yet exist. A leader creates a vision, gives people the means to achieve it, tracks results, and rewards successes. Great leaders put missteps behind them and redirect when necessary. They live the philosophy, "We don't make mistakes; we make adjustments."

Track:
How Do We Know
This Is Working?

I love numbers, which would come as a surprise to my high school math teacher. Intuition is certainly valuable, and often underrated in business, but when it comes to evaluating a process and deciding on adjustments, you have to have numbers. Without a means of tracking the success of the Three Big Words you risk putting energy in the wrong direction. The challenge is that some areas of business are easily tracked with numbers, sales and manufacturing, while others seem entirely reliant on intuition, relationships, satisfaction. To this point, a friend of mine was getting his MBA and had just finished a course in statistics. When I asked him the greatest lesson he learned from the class he said, "I learned that you can create a metrics for everything." In business, even non-tangibles must be tracked.

I was asked to work with a global printing operation. The director of one division noticed that his staff had become overly reliant on texting and e-mailing clients instead of picking up the phone and having a conversation. My workshop was meant to help the staff not only see the importance of voice-to-voice, or face-to-face communication, but feel confident they could handle difficult conversations. The main reason why many of them used text instead of voice communication was that they had to deliver bad news to a client. E-mail is certainly an easier way to deliver bad news, but the practice is ultimately self-defeating because hearing bad news through text just makes the news feel even worse. Only your voice can soothe a bad situation.

After the workshop the director wanted to know how we could keep the momentum going. He was justifiably concerned that his staff would convert to face-to-face conversation immediately following the workshop but eventually slip back into old habits. I asked, "Do you have a method of tracking how many times an employee calls a client versus texting or e-mail?" The director had no such system in place; not surprising since such a tracking method is not typical in most companies. However, in order to create positive change, a tracking method would be a necessary next step in order to create long-term results. Before we could continue with further training, the directors had to devise a simple and effective way of tracking how many times a staff member used the phone instead of texting or e-mailing a client.

In the book, *Seven Measures of Success*, the authors used the methodology behind the book, *Good to Great* to analyze the success of member-driven, non-profit organizations. *Good to Great* compared successful companies with organizations in similar industries that didn't enjoy the same success. *Seven Measures of Success* did the same thing for the world of member-driven associations. For instance, there are hundreds of non-profit organizations that serve senior citizens, but AARP is the biggest. In fact, as of the publishing of *Seven Measures of Success* in 2006, AARP is the largest membership-based non-profit organization in the world.

What the researchers found were seven areas in which successful organizations did things differently. The first measure of success is *Be data driven, not assumption driven*, relates well to the issue of this chapter; tracking and measuring success rather than assuming things are going well. It is all too common for business leaders to make assumptions instead of relying on evidence. They assume what the customer or client wants, assume what will make staff members happy, and assume that a certain way of doing things is "The right way to do it, of course." The problem is that things can flow along smoothly for quite a while, allowing us to assume that the success is due to one thing when, in fact, it is due to another. Many companies succeed in spite of their actions, not because of them.

Great organizations ask themselves "How do we know?" And when they get the answer, they double-check it with "How do we *know* we know?" One of the reasons AARP is the granddaddy (no pun intended) of senior service organizations is that they constantly verify their facts. To do this, they rely on the most reliable source of information available to any company, their customers. AARP members are constantly surveyed. Every month a new survey is sent to seniors asking about their feelings and preferences. Since AARP has so many members, even though the membership is constantly being surveyed, a particular member may only be surveyed once, or not at all, but the sample size of each survey still ensures accuracy. And the philosophy at AARP is "Never question or dismiss the survey results." Many organizations dismiss feedback from customers, members, or clients by claiming that "the customer doesn't know the whole story" or "they don't represent our *real* client." These are great excuses, and they make sure the company doesn't have to change. The excuses don't help when the company has no idea why sales have fallen. At AARP the rule is, "If the majority of members want us to do something a certain way that is the way we do it; no questions asked."

AARP has so many members that they can survey to their heart's content without worrying about calling on the same member too many times for input. Smaller companies, of course, must foster the kind of relationship in which the customer or client feels like a trusted advisor. Achieving this kind of relationship isn't easy, and too many companies try to achieve it through tricks or gimmicks. In my home state, the electric company is part of a large conglomerate. The company recently decided to solicit input from its customers. One day I received an e-mail invitation to become part of "an exclusive team of people" who would receive regular surveys about our electric service. As an incentive, every time you completed a survey your name would be entered into a drawing to receive a gift card to a local restaurant or store.

On its face, the reward of a gift card for participation seems like a nice incentive, but on a deeper level it demonstrates a lack of understanding of what truly motivates people. People offer feedback because they either want to feel important, they want to correct a problem, or they want to be part of a solution. Bribing people with a gift card can result in lack-luster participation and inaccurate feedback. And, after the customer has completed a few dozen surveys and has yet to win anything, the initial excitement of being part of a special team is replaced by resentment toward the company.

Also, a survey (or whatever means of tracking you employ), relies on honest feedback; feedback that the provider is sure will help improve something, not simply to help the company make more money. For example, a short time after joining the electric company's special team I received my first online survey. It asked me to select one of three advertising campaigns—complete with slogans, posters, and billboards—as my favorite. All three campaigns had the same goal, get the public to support the electric company's goal to begin charging a special fee to customers who owned solar panels. Essentially, the electric company didn't like losing revenue to people with solar panels, so they wanted to make money by assessing special fees, but needed public support to attain government approval.

This survey wasn't to gain my insight into how to make the world a better place. It wasn't to improve the electric service to me and my neighbors. And it was not meant to solve a problem I was facing, it was meant to improve the bottom line of the electric company. It was a not-so veiled attempt to increase revenue. (I was biased in my responses to this survey because my wife and I were the first house in our city to install rooftop solar panels. That, along with converting to LED lighting, lowered our electric usage from the grid by 90%. I think if the electric company had known that, I would been left off that particular survey.) Be that as it may, even a customer without a stake in the game can smell deceit. If a survey is meant to gain honest feedback, most people are excited to offer comments. If a company is disguising a self-serving motive under the title of "Survey," forget it. Of course, customers know that every company is concerned with sales and profits. Feedback from customers, however, must be connected to something more meaningful.

Another example; many restaurant managers are coached to track the guest experience by strolling around the dining area; stopping at tables and asking, "How is everything tonight folks?" This is another ineffective means of gaining feedback. First of all, if something is wrong with the meal, I should be talking to the person who brought it to me, my server. If I haven't told my server something is wrong, why would I tell a stranger who just walked up to my table? Second; no manager has yet to approach me in a way that would elicit honest feedback. The phrase, "How is everything tonight, folks?" is not a request for feedback; it is essentially asking the guest to reply, "Everything is fine." If, instead, a restaurant manager approached me and said, "Hi. My name is Andre, I'm the manager here. I noticed you ordered the walleye. If you don't mind me asking, we have been trying a new recipe for the fish and I would love your opinion. Is it spicy enough or does it need more of a kick?" Remember Ben, the head of security for the Mall of America? In order to gain honest feedback from a guest, he engaged in honest conversation. He said to a guest,

"You look like a really observant person. I would love to hear your observations about the mall." He didn't ask, "Is everything going okay?" As a result he came away with more great ideas to improve the mall than any survey could provide. Asking questions and engaging in conversation always beats a survey. The reason companies use surveys instead is because surveys are cheaper, easier, and can reach a broad audience. Companies have fooled themselves into thinking that, as long as they survey enough people, the statistics will bear fruit. If you survey 1,000 people and get 1,000 half-hearted, untruthful responses, the sample size doesn't matter. And simplicity that results in poor feedback isn't any better. As far as expense, conversations are free.

There is another reason why companies use the easy approach of online surveys, they don't really want the truth. If you engage in honest conversation with an employee or a customer, you are likely to hear about areas where the company is falling down on the job. The reason leaders don't like to hear bad news is not due to a character flaw; it is because of the way our brains are wired. It is a psychological fact that humans seek information that will support a previously held belief; this is called *confirmation bias*. Confirmation bias is a part of our psyche that keeps us safe from bad news by allowing us to ignore painful truths. It also allows us to continue on a familiar path; and if there is one thing the human brain doesn't like, it is having to change behavior. AARP eliminated the risk on confirmation bias by establishing a rule that no statistics would ever be questioned. You may utilize one-on-one interviews, but they support the *what* by providing the *why*. In any case, no AARP employee is allowed to dismiss a customer concern by making an excuse for the way things are done, by claiming that the customer's concern is an anomaly, or by claiming that the customer doesn't have enough insight into the company to make a judgement.

A number of years ago a group of director-level executives met with me to discuss working with their company to improve employee morale. Low morale was creating high turn-over, low productivity…you know the story. When I met with the directors, the CEO was conspicuously absent. The directors said that the CEO had previously hired a firm that specialized in corporate culture. When this consulting firm completed their examination of the company, they held a meeting with the CEO and all the directors. They reported that their research revealed that the entire organization was managed under a culture of fear. Every employee, from new hires to seasoned veterans, was unable to do his or her best work because they were constantly afraid of some kind of punishment or reprisal. When they said the organization operated under a veil of fear, the CEO interrupted them, stood up, slammed his fist on the table and screamed, "No, it is not!" That was one of only two companies I have ever declined to work with.

Fast forward three years. I was meeting with another company experiencing low productivity and high turn-over. As you might expect, the lack of employee engagement also resulted in poor customer service. The only path to customer loyalty is an engaged workforce. Over the few weeks that I met with the owner and his executive team I detailed the research that I used as the basis of my work. Quite a bit of the information was the result of cutting edge studies, so they contradicted age-old beliefs in how to best manage employees and run a business. After I finished describing a particularly relevant study that would apply to his business, the owner said, "Well, that's all good on paper, but in the real world…" His was the other business I declined to work with.

Then there was the senior executive who called me into her office to discuss the work I was conducting with her company. I was warned by her staff to expect a lot of resistance to my work; not because my concepts were too far-fetched, but because she cut down any idea that wasn't hers. Sure enough, when we met she openly admitted that the reason she would be "your biggest obstacle" is because she had tried to initiate a similar program a year earlier and had been shot down. My ideas were fine, they just weren't her ideas. I did end up working with her, but only after some long conversations to eliminate her confirmation bias.

Companies think that creating the next best idea is the greatest challenge they face. The real challenge is battling confirmation bias. Look at politics. If someone is a staunch Republican, any evidence that a Democrat has done a worthy deed is dismissed. If someone is a steadfast Democrat, a Republican will be vilified for any offense, even if a Democrat committed the same mistake. Even the world of medicine has been slow to improve because of confirmation bias. Physicians have relied on intuition to diagnosis illnesses for so long that when new evidence suggested their methods are flawed, the evidence is doubted; not their own practice.

It isn't the lack of new ideas or evidence that is most costly to businesses; it is the unwillingness to accept evidence that challenges our firmly held beliefs. Businesses spend tens of thousands of dollars each year searching for the next best practice, or to seek out weak spots in their organization; only to have the results buried on a shelf because the findings made someone feel uncomfortable, or because the report challenged deeply rooted beliefs. Evidence does us no good if we are unwilling to put it to use.

To create positive change, we must first ask ourselves what we are willing to give up in order to get the outcome we desire. When psychologists counsel patients who are stuck in destructive patterns, the first question they seek to answer is what payoff is the patient getting from the behavior? Often, even though the behavior itself is destructive, it is more comfortable to deal with the consequences of the bad behavior than to venture into uncharted territory. Some people fear that admitting it is time to change is tantamount to admitting they were doing it wrong in the first place. Not true. The ability to change in the face of new information is a sign of advanced intelligence. Pessimism and doubt are low-intelligence behaviors. Like Einstein said, *"No problem can be solved from the same level of consciousness that created it."*

This is not to suggest that anecdotal evidence should replace facts and figures; far from it. Both methods should be used to support the other. Statistics are the facts, conversation tells you the why. The reason surveys are inaccurate at telling you the why is because you are asking people to remember a past experience, and human memory is flawed. You then ask people to give reasons why they feel a certain way or decide to do a certain thing. Since people act based on emotions instead of pure reasoning or logic, in order to finish the survey they must create plausible reasons to justify their feelings. The only time a survey like this has any degree of accuracy is if the survey is taken immediately after the experience; so the memory of the experience is fresh. However, even though our memory of the experience might be accurate, the tendency to justify feelings with plausible facts is still present.

Numbers do tell a story, if you are willing to listen. Some years ago, my company employed a business communications expert to take a look at how we engaged our company members and students. She was an outsider so she had no stake in the outcome of the process, as such people were willing to be honest with her. Giving negative feedback to a company member can be uncomfortable, so it is easier to just say what the person wants to hear. After she finished interviewing a good chunk of our population she reported that our company members felt a great deal of connection with the organization and its leaders, but only after being with the company for four months or more. From the time of joining until the four-month mark, we were at the greatest risk of losing people due to them feeling disconnected from the company. Those are the kind of numbers that are valuable. It allowed us to create methods of connecting with new members right away. The numbers we received from her report were not a threat; but an opportunity.

When creating a tracking system, an important consideration is tracking the right thing. A great example comes from Jan Carlzon. At the age of 36, Carlzon became the world's youngest airline president when he took over Sweden's domestic airline, Linjeflyg. As a result of his leading the airline in an incredible turn-around, he was made president of Scandinavian Airlines (SAS). Again, he led SAS to record growth, profits, and customer/employee satisfaction. Along the way he learned a number of lessons about tracking results. When the airline wanted to improve the cargo shipping part of the business, they examined their reports and determined that they were doing very well on the most important metric for shipping cargo: precision. On paper, almost 100% of cargo items arrived at their destination on time. However, Carlzon was suspicious. Even with the positive results, the cargo division wasn't experiencing the growth that would follow such success. He decided to test SAS tracking methods by sending 100 parcels throughout Europe and tracking their arrival times. The results were astonishing. Rather than arriving next day, as expected, most arrived days later. The tracking system used was inaccurate because the paperwork only tracked whether items were shipped on the correct flight and if the item arrived; period. A glitch in the paperwork made some items appear to arrive on time when, in fact, they did not. Carlzon said, "We had caught ourselves in one of the most basic mistakes a service-oriented business can make: promising one thing and measuring another." Once they changed the tracking method to reflect whether promises were actually being fulfilled, outcomes improved dramatically. You can read more about this in his book, *Moments of Truth*.

Carlzon did something else that many companies do not; he shared information with the entire staff. Many companies will track results only to keep the information hidden up in the C-level offices. The big-wigs think that because they are the decision makers, they should be the only ones privy to this top-secret information; a classic attitude toward front-line staff, "We don't pay you to think." Yes, some leaders still use that ridiculous phrase. If you share information with the entire staff, as well as engage them in the big goals of the company, they will be your best source of ideas for growth and improvement. The only thing that needs to get out of the way is the ego of those at the top. Carlzon made sure that all survey results and efficiency reports were shared company-wide. The ideas for solutions that his staff provided were invaluable. The practice actually made the job of a C-level executive a lot easier.

Tracking is, at its core, all about giving everyone a scorecard. My wife, Kanitta, my step-daughter, Ondine, and I love to play miniature golf (which is, by the way, the only time you will see a golf club in my hand). Ondine loves to be the one to keep score; I think she got that trait from her mother. As soon as we all finish with one hole, she grabs the scorecard and marks everyone down. I think she likes it so much because she always beats me and Kanitta by a wide margin. I'm sure that mini-golf would be just as fun without keeping score, but there would definitely be something missing. It reminds me of an episode of *Star Trek: The Next Generation.* Some crew members are leaving to play a highly competitive game against another ship. The character of Captain Picard reminds them to enjoy the game for its own sake; that winning isn't everything. One crew member replies, "If winning isn't important, why keep score?"

A scorecard of some kind for every employee is a means of reminding them what they are there to accomplish. It isn't something to hold over their head and pull out during an employee evaluation. It isn't a threat, it is a motivator. A scorecard of some kind provides a constant reminder, but it also makes improvement more of a game and less of a chore. If managers and employees work together to create an appropriate scorecard method, you take the fear out of having a scorecard. Winning doesn't always mean there is a loser. Improving upon one's personal best is enough. And make sure you have a scorecard for every employee, especially the tough-to-track ones. A sales staff is easy to measure, so are litigators; how much revenue did you generate or how many cases did you win? Find a way to give a scorecard to staff members whose work is not so easily quantified and you will get a more engaged employee. And a more engaged employee builds loyal customers.

"An individual without information cannot take responsibility; an individual who is given information cannot help but take responsibility."

> Jan Carlzon
> President, Scandinavian Airlines

Maintain: Don't Be the Flavor of the Month

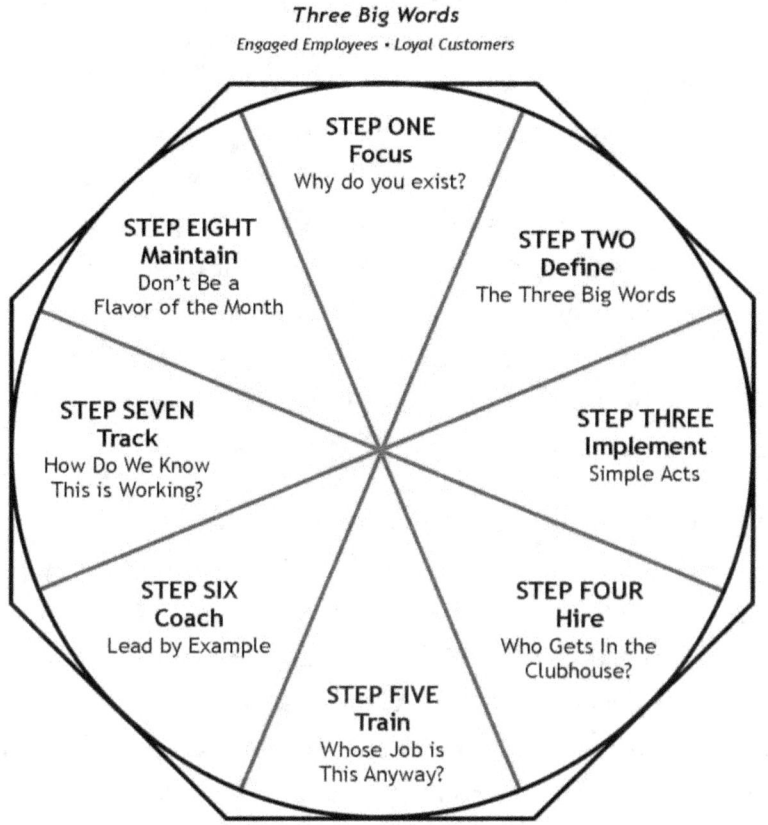

It might sound strange that a guy who wrote this book, promoting long-term culture change, also admits that having flavor-of-the-month programs isn't necessarily a bad thing when it comes to employee engagement. I know employees can sometimes roll their eyes when management rolls out the next "exciting program," but there is a downside to completely abandoning such efforts. When I am working with a company to set up training, I will usually ask what kind of programs they have run before. The response includes the usual list of whatever is hot at the moment. One year it was Myers-Briggs, the next year was DISC, the next was your "personal leadership color," and so on. It is easy to dismiss all of these because they seem to come and go, but let's be realistic. If every employee absorbed every concept from every workshop and employed the new techniques at work, it would make for a pretty confusing workplace.

The reason so many different programs and theories exist is not because each one is the perfect choice for every company and every employee, it is because human beings are so complex that you need to offer a range of approaches and have each employee decide what to keep and what to discard. The reason having a flavor of the month works for ice cream parlors is precisely the same reason it works for the workplace—variety. Even if vanilla is the best way to run your company you still need to offer Rocky Road or Cherry Garcia every now and then just to keep things interesting. This book is meant to provide the foundation for long-term focus, employee engagement, and growth. It is meant to be the vanilla upon which you add nuts, chocolate chips, whipped cream, or whatever else seems interesting. The Three Big Words is not meant to replace every other training or engagement program, it is meant to work alongside them. If anyone accuses you of offering another *flavor of the month*, tell them "Darn right! And wouldn't life be dull if I didn't?"

That said, the most difficult part of the Three Big Words process is keeping the momentum going. Whenever I am asked to conduct a workshop the client invariably asks, "How do we know that the staff isn't just going to go back to doing things the old way?" Many organizations get stuck in the trap of trying several different programs and, after an initial period of excitement and change, things go back to business as usual. It is common to blame the program itself for lack of staying power, and indeed there are hundreds of consultants and trainers who over-promise and under-deliver. It is unfair, however, to expect the kind of results some leaders expect when they simply "throw a workshop" at the problem and wait for everything to fall in place.

The first step in maintaining positive change is actually quite simple: create an atmosphere where change is expected instead of just hoped for. This might seem simple enough, but I mention it because of the number of times I have encountered leaders who were actually afraid of their own employees. At one company, I had conducted training sessions for all the employee groups and everyone seemed excited about the new direction. They understood the one reason the organization existed, were clear on the Three Big Words, and felt comfortable with the Simple Acts. At a follow-up meeting with the department heads, I was discussing how to keep the momentum going and a department manager asked me, "What do we do if the employees don't want to follow the plan?" I paused and asked, "Since when is it their choice?"

This company was by no means unsuccessful, but they called me because they wanted to help the staff feel better connected and build morale. After meeting with the directors, I learned of a few challenges the company faced. Most employees were so isolated from leadership that they couldn't pick the CEO out of a line-up (not that you *want* your CEO in a line-up). Also, the department heads rarely met as a group. The attitude seemed to be that, as long as everyone did his or her job, everything was fine and there was no need to waste everyone's time with pointless meetings. Granted, a lot of meetings can be a waste of time, but the practice of each department head meeting only with one or two leaders at the very top—and never meeting with each other—encourages hoarding. The CEO meets with one department at a time and gathers information from each. This allows the CEO to hoard the information at the top. The CEO can then dole out assignments without any cross communication between departments. This is common in business (and governments); it makes the leaders feel justified in their position. Rather than empower other leaders in the company to solve problems together, the CEO puts him/herself in the position of Chief Problem Solver. This is a great way to feed the ego, but a lousy use of available talent and wisdom. Another outcome of this practice is an atmosphere of distrust between departments.

In the case of this company, the other outcome was a lack of a unified front when leadership brought new initiatives to the staff. From the very first meeting, I could tell that those in charge were nervous about introducing any new idea to the staff for fear it would meet resistance. If I discussed a point in the program that might either add to an employee's work load or be a change from the status quo, it was harder to get the management team on board than to deal with the staff.

It reminded me of a time years earlier when I was a jury foreman for a criminal trial. We were to decide the guilt or innocence of a defendant charged with a violent act against a vulnerable adult—a senior citizen with Alzheimer's disease. The deliberation was tense because the crime, being violent as well as committed against a vulnerable person, carried a stiff sentence. The evidence was conclusive and all but two jurors had voted guilty in the poll we conducted. At one point Sheila, one of those two jurors, said "All right. I see your point. I'll vote guilty, but I won't like it." At this point the remaining jurors started to protest, saying that she shouldn't vote guilty if she wasn't comfortable. I spoke up saying, "Wait. It is not our job to make sure everyone feels good about the choice they make here today. Frankly, I don't think any of us should. I haven't had a full night's sleep since the trial began. Making the right choice isn't always easy, even if it feels right. Sheila is an adult and it isn't our job to make her feel one way or the other. If she thinks the man is guilty, that is how she should vote. If not, then she should remain in the non-guilty camp; either way, the choice is hers and so are the consequences of that choice." Managers have the same task, make a choice because it is the right thing to do. If some staff members don't like the decision, they must learn that following directions is part of the job.

The department managers suggested soliciting input from the staff as we developed the program, which I always think is a good idea. The problem is the directors were less interested in learning about the thoughts of the staff and more interested in trying to gain full consensus before moving ahead with any decision. While gaining input is valuable, consensus is rarely possible. When was the last time you and a few friends could decide where to go to lunch in less than half an hour? Most people are reasonable; they know that the vote isn't always going to go their way. As long as employees have input, and are genuinely heard, they will be okay with the final decision. I said to the department heads, "When you board a plane you certainly don't expect all the passengers to vote on the destination. You learn about the destination at the gate and then decide if that is the right plane for you to board. The airline company decides the destination and the pilot makes sure the plane follows the directive of the company. Likewise, you don't ask your staff if they want to employ new directives. You tell them what is expected of them and give them all the help you can so they can be successful at it. Once the company decides on a new direction, the employees should expect help from managers so they can be successful, but they don't get a vote as to whether the initiative is to be followed."

Being afraid of how employees would react to decisions is what my business partner, Pamela Mayne, and I call *being held hostage by the staff*. It has taken many years and many painful lessons for us to learn that working relationships are no different than personal ones. One harmful trait in any relationship is co-dependency. If you make decisions that are against your best interests, but you do so in order to please someone else, that is co-dependent behavior. And there is a big difference between being kind and being co-dependent. If you buy your spouse flowers because you know it will make him or her happy, that is a kindness. If you buy flowers because you are afraid you will get yelled at if you don't, that is co-dependent.

It is folly to make decisions in an attempt to make someone happy. Happiness comes from within each individual, not the circumstances in which they find themselves. If a person is happy, they will experience occasional bouts of sadness or disappointment, but they will generally stay emotionally level. If a person is ultimately unhappy, he or she will blame circumstances; not their life choices. Circumstances can make us satisfied or disappointed, but ultimate happiness has nothing to do with external forces. Pamela and I have been held hostage by our own employees on several occasions. When we examine past decisions it is easy to see when we were trying to make someone happy instead of doing the right thing. We have kept people on the payroll long after they should have been asked to leave, and we have placed people in positions because of the opinions of others instead of following our own instincts. One example of a co-dependent decision we made regarded Hank.

Hank had been a member of our resident performance company for about two years. The resident performance company is the troupe that performs at our cabaret each weekend. Hank was the music director and would accompany the show at the piano. When he first started with our company he was every manager's dream. He never complained, offered to do more than was asked, and treated the rest of the company with respect. However, after a couple of years things took a turn for the worse. Even though he worked for us, Hank had a few other irons in the fire. We made it clear that his work with us had to be his first priority. In the beginning, this was no problem, but soon he was asking for so many nights off that he was working only about two thirds of his scheduled performances. We had some conversations with him about his commitment and he promised to do better.

About two months after our "renew your commitment" meeting, Hank presented us with another list of nights he would need to miss. It was back to the same old problem. We didn't make the right choice right away. We allowed ourselves to reminisce about how great he was in the beginning, about how he was a nice guy, and we talked about wishing for the old Hank to come back. After a while, we realized that we had forgotten the advice therapists give couples going through a split, "You never divorce the person you married. They are a different person now, and so are you. Move on." Hank was not the same person that we first hired; that version of Hank was not coming back.

We also let guilt creep into the conversation. We talked about how firing Hank could affect his financial situation. We also worried about the other company members. Would they be sorry to see their friend fired? In the end, we came to our senses and realized that, if Hank really needed the money he would find a way to commit to his position with us. And if the other members would be sad to see him go, imagine how much sadder they would feel not having bosses who stuck to their principles. But here is where the co-dependent attitude really came in. But even after this realization, we acted in a co-dependent manner. Rather than simply having Hank move on, we decided to offer him the music director position with our touring company. While the resident company performs every weekend, the touring company is hired on an as-needed basis. We thought this was a perfect solution to the problem of Hank's crowded schedule. He would be free to pursue other opportunities and still be able to play for us for corporate performances and private events. It seemed a perfect solution for everyone, except it wasn't.

Had Pamela and I taken a step back we would have realized that we weren't offering Hank the touring company position because he was the right fit, we did it to placate him. Why would any leader take someone who had displayed such disrespect and lack of cooperation and offer him another position within the company? Although Hank acted grateful to our face when offered the new position, he spent his remaining weeks in the resident company making the rest of the members miserable. He pouted, gave people the silent treatment, and on his last night he delivered a diatribe about how he was mistreated by the company. Throughout the years Pamela and I have constantly reminded each other that our decisions must be for the good of the company, but we failed when it came to Hank. Instead of one clean break, where Hank went his was and we went ours, we dragged out the process, and dragged the company members through it as well. We ended up having to fire him altogether, which would have been the right choice at the start.

The first step to maintaining the Three Big Words program is to create an air of expectation, not demand. Management must show the staff that they are excited and committed to the new direction, and will expect nothing less than total commitment. The next step is to make sure your expectations are reasonable. Nothing kills enthusiasm more quickly than prolonged failure. Occasional setbacks may build resiliency and determination, but if someone knows they will never reach the top of a mountain, they would be foolish to keep climbing. An old colleague of mine, Dr. Frank Freedman, was hired as a consultant for a company. As he was discussing their objectives, the client continued to heap on problem after problem that they wanted Frank to fix. The frosting on the cake was when they said that they could only allot a one-day session for the entire program. Dr. Frank looked at the client with a straight face and said, "I'll only need the morning. I usually keep the afternoon open so I can cure world hunger." After the laughter died down, everyone got back to talking about the program, but with more realistic expectations.

At another conference, I listened to the CEO of a big box electronics retail chain. One of his *Ten Rules for Success* was "Some years, just staying open is a success." His presentation was delivered in 2011 during the height of the recession. Retail was being hit hard. He said he couldn't understand business leaders who beat up their staff to achieve double-digit growth during a time when hundreds of companies were struggling just to keep their doors open.

A one-time presentation or workshop is referred to as a "one-off," or a "one-and-done." This type of presentation is perfect for learning some quick new techniques or infusing a little energy in the group. Seeing the same faces every day, year after year, is enough to dull the senses and sap the energy out of any working group. Hearing from an outsider offers a new perspective and can re-focus a group. Sometimes even hearing the same old message from someone new, or in a new way, is enough to provide a spark. One-and-done sessions are fine, but make sure you ground your expectations in reality. If you need a whole-sale shift in attitudes or practices, prepare for a marathon, not a sprint.

Once you have created an atmosphere of expectation and have set reasonable goals, you need to get some champions behind the idea. The notion of an *Idea Champion* is not new. Those who coach business growth and product development know that ideas come and go, but those that survive are the ones that have someone behind them; someone to help the idea survive the inevitable nay-sayers and obstacles. If you recall from the book *Influencer: The Power to Change Anything*, one key element in making drastic changes for large organizations is to employ the help of opinion leader*s*; people who may not hold rank in the company, but whose opinion holds sway among the staff. Watch employees after a typical meeting and they are likely to hover around one of their colleagues and ask "So what do you think about all this?" If you want to maintain the success of the Three Big Words, get opinion leaders on board first.

You also can't have long-term success without two important elements: *regular reminders* and *cross-communication*. Departments that don't talk to anyone outside their sphere are in danger of slipping back into old habits. More importantly, employees need to see how other people in the company are doing with new initiatives. Hearing success stories from other employees provides two important things: 1) it assures them that they too can have success, 2) it creates an expectation of their participation. Essentially, getting employees to commit to a long-term goal doesn't just rely on a successful plan and good leadership; it relies on a social network.

Here are some methods other companies have used to make the social network principle work for them:

A dry erase board is mounted by the employee entrance or break room. As employees check-out at the end of their shift or eat lunch, they are encouraged to share success stories from their day. If an employee came upon a creative solution to a guest's problem, or learned a valuable lesson while helping a customer or fellow employee, this is a fantastic way to not only pass along that knowledge the fellow employees, but it also provides a daily reminder. Messages like these carry more weight because they come from fellow employees. Authority figures certainly have valuable insights to share, but the effectiveness of their message greatly depends on how much trust the employee has in the leader. A message from a fellow employee feels less like a command, and is also more motivating. The message comes across less like "You should do it" and more like "We can do this." This practice is, of course, easily modified for companies that don't have a central employee gathering place. Employee-to-employee messages can become part of a company-wide newsletter or intranet system.

If you recall from the beginning of the book the research about *Distributed Teams*—working groups that are scattered geographically—the best way to maintain morale and engagement is communication that is both frequent and spontaneous. The reason having a dry erase board in the break room is a good idea is because employees have frequent opportunities to contribute stories, but it is not an overly-regulated process. If you send e-mail newsletters on a weekly or monthly basis, the messages lose impact because they lack spontaneity. Employees open the e-mail with an attitude of "here we go with another motivational story." Giving employees a chance to share their own stories is both frequent and spontaneous.

I can speak to the effect of spontaneity on inspiration in my own work. As a columnist for the Business Journal newspapers, I have a deadline on the second Friday of every month. If I put off writing the column until that morning I usually sit staring at a blank screen. Those columns aren't usually my best work. So instead, I make it a practice to remember moments that strongly affect me, either as a customer or a trainer. As long as I can recall real-world experiences to share with readers, I am never short of ideas for my column. The same strategy that has provided staying power for my writing can work to provide staying power for the Three Big Words.

Moments that make you feel, that provide strong emotions, provide inspiration. Sharing stories of inspiration in frequent and spontaneous ways with others in the company is a great way to drive momentum. If you don't have a common gathering place for employees, use technology. Inter- or intranet sharing sites, e-mail blasts, or employee-created videos are simple methods of maintaining focus and motivation.

You might have noticed something different about the methods of maintaining momentum I have described so far;

they are driven from the bottom, not the top. For generations, companies have generated marching orders from leadership. Managers are charged with delivering those orders to the staff, and then enforcing those orders. In any such system, where input from staff is minimal, there is inherent resistance from front-line employees. It has nothing to do with the quality of the idea or the ability of the staff to manage change in the workplace. When change is ordered from the top, managed from the middle, and instituted at the bottom, motivation is bound to be short-lived. This is why most large-scale changes ultimately fail. For real change to occur, C-level executives must let front-line employees sit in the driver's seat. You have to let opinion leaders within the ranks give their stamp of approval. Change must be driven from the bottom up or it is doomed.

This means that assigning cheerleaders to motivate staff will also fail. An opinion leader is a person the employees trust and respect, not just someone who is confident and believes in the initiative. One company I worked with was committed to having a new customer service plan take hold among the employees, so they assigned Chloe from the marketing department to be the idea champion. As I mentioned earlier, most new initiatives will fail without an idea champion; someone with the wherewithal, authority, and passion to see it through to completion. This doesn't mean that those are the only three qualities that matter. Chloe had a bubbly energetic personality, so the company leaders thought she would be the perfect idea champion. What they didn't take into account was that while everyone liked Chloe and enjoyed her company, they didn't respect her as a leader. Her cheerleading approach turned people off. Instead of championing the idea, she was a big part of the reason it sunk.

Another concept Robert Cialdini writes about in *Influence: Science and Practice* is the power of commitment and consistency. In order to get employees to maintain a new initiative, leaders must achieve deep commitment on the part of employees, and then create an atmosphere where the employee's words demand consistent behavior. One of the best ways to do this is through a simple signature. A conversation between a manager and an employee is okay, but it doesn't often result in full commitment on the part of the employee. This is because the spoken word is here and gone. This is why contracts are so effective. Written contracts are not simply to get details on paper so there is no confusion later, it is to get a signature from both parties. Something magical happens when we put our signature on a document. We are now committed to following through on a promise. Family therapists recommend having parents create a contract for behavior for their children. A child who signs a document agreeing not to engage in bad behavior is many times more likely to honor the agreement than a child who simply offers a verbal agreement. Consider having employees sign a contract agreeing to abide by the principles of the Three Big Words.

If you want to gain commitment on a larger scale, consider going one step further–public commitment. Cialdini recounts tactics used by the Chinese during the Korean War to influence the behavior of American POWs. Rather than pressure American soldiers to turn against their country or fellow soldiers, the Chinese employed sophisticated psychological maneuvers. They would first ask a question for which there was only one answer, "We know that China isn't perfect. You certainly don't think America is perfect, do you?" If the soldier agreed, the Chinese would take the next step, "If you truly believe that, then you shouldn't mind writing that down." If the soldier wrote on a piece of paper that America wasn't perfect, the Chinese would ask him to list a few for-examples about America's imperfection. Because the human brain is wired with an in-for-a-penny, in-for-a-pound mentality, taking the next step wasn't a big leap; most POWs complied. Then the Chinese asked for the most important step of all, "If you said it, and you wrote it, you must believe in it. So you shouldn't have a problem signing it." Most soldiers signed their statement, believing that would be the end of it. However, the Chinese would then post the statements around the POW camp for other American soldiers to see. The outcome was something few military experts would expect. Even though American soldiers were fervently patriotic as well as loyal to their fellow POWs, soldiers began turning in other soldiers who were trying to escape the camp. This happened due to a confluence of commitment and consistency.

When we sign our name to a document, we become committed to its contents, but even more impact is felt by our social circle. When other people see our name on a document, they believe that we stand behind those statements. In an experiment discussed in *Influence: Science and Practice*, people were shown a document with a signature. When asked if they thought the person who wrote the document believed in what he wrote, they said yes. Another group of people were given the same signed document, but they were told that the person who wrote it was forced at gunpoint to write and sign it. When asked if they thought he believed what he wrote, almost all participants still said yes. When other soldiers saw signed documents around the POW camp, they naturally believed that a fellow soldier was speaking against America. As a result, they turned against the soldier who wrote the document. The outcast soldiers were the ones who turned in other American soldiers.

You might ask, "Wouldn't an outcast try to prove his loyalty by working even harder to help his fellow POWs?" That would be the case if it wasn't for an important function of the brain—consistency. If we are told often enough that we are a certain kind of person, we will become that person. Our behavior must be consistent with our world view. Most of us can remember a time when, as a child, we thought "Fine. If they think I stole the cookie I am going to steal cookies every day from now on." That type of thinking isn't just the ranting of an indignant child, it is the function of the human brain. Once the soldiers were, in a sense, separated from their comrades, and given the identity of "helping the Chinese," they had no option but to remain consistent with that identity.

Behaving consistent with identity is affected by the smallest choice of words. In a studies conducted at Boston College and the University of Houston, two groups of people participated in an experiment to limit consumption of red meat. When offered meat at a meal, one group would say the phrase, "I *can't* eat red meat." The other group would say the phrase, "I *don't* eat red meat." The group that said *don't* instead of *can't* were much more successful at sticking to a vegetarian diet. The word *don't* implies an identity, the word *can't* speaks to a rule. People naturally resist rules, but they uphold an identity.

I am certainly not suggesting you do anything as manipulative as the Chinese did in the POW camps, but there are respectful and effective ways to establish commitment and consistency in your company as you seek to maintain the Three Big Words. Have employees sign agreements concerning the Simple Acts. If you post success stories about employees, include a signature in order to attach commitment to behavior. Don't be afraid to use the public sphere of the workplace to provide healthy influence. The Chinese used the public sphere to shame and isolate, you can use it to encourage camaraderie and mutual support.

Whatever methods you choose to maintain the momentum of the Three Big Words, it must include communication among the staff that is frequent, spontaneous, and employee-driven. The most important part of maintaining any initiative is to keep performing small steps. Don't focus all your energy on one big push and then hope inertia will take care of the rest. As the old Chinese saying goes, *It doesn't matter how slow you move, as long as you keep walking.*

Final Thoughts

There you have it. The simplest—and most difficult—process to realign the vision of your organization, engage employees, and create loyal customers. It is simple because the concepts that make up the Three Big Words are fairly easy to understand. It is difficult because it takes a lot of work to make it work. For some organizations, just deciding on the *one reason you exist* can cause fierce debates. For others, the Three Big Words can take weeks to figure out. I have seen business leaders dig in their heels in heated discussions over using the word *honest* instead of *trusted*. Such debates are a good sign, it demonstrates a commitment to take the process seriously and get it right. The Three Big Words will create a new culture within your organization. And because this new culture will be defined by the very core of your organization's beliefs and values, it shouldn't change–ever. So, take the time to get it right before rolling it out to your staff.

Now go find Emma.

About the Author

Stephen "Stevie Ray" Rentfrow was born a small boy, which worked out so well he decided to remain one. Stevie co-founded *Stevie Ray's Improv Company* in 1989 and continues to run it with his partner, Pamela Mayne. He is a nationally syndicated columnist for the Business Journal Newspapers, a corporate trainer, and keynote speaker.

Stevie Ray is the only person in the country to design his own college degree, *Theory and Performance of Comedy* (his parents were *so* proud). He has he toured the country performing with such stars as "Weird Al" Yankovic, Paula Poundstone, Marsha Warfield of *Night Court,* and Rich Hall of *Saturday Night Live*. He is a lot funnier on stage than he is in this book.

A martial artist since 1977, he has studied seven martial arts and holds four black belts in four of them. At one point in his career he was a bodyguard for Pee Wee Herman (yes, really).

Stevie is also a beekeeper and producer of *Steve's Bees Minnesota Honey* and a volunteer for the Minnesota State Services for the Blind, recording books on tape for the blind.

Stevie lives in Minneapolis with his wife, Kanitta and step-daughter, Ondine.

Other books by Stevie Ray

About the Rent
One Thousand Punches a Day
Quick Thinking for Any Situation
Speaking in Public without Sweating in Private
Spontaneity Takes Practice
The Birth, Life, (and sometimes death), of a Comedian
The Calm Before the Brainstorm
What We Laugh At... and Why
Working the Room: Networking for Professionals

www.ingramcontent.com/pod-product-compliance
Lightning Source LLC
Chambersburg PA
CBHW052148220526
45471CB00004B/1577